40 Que Jesus ASKS

40 Questions
Jesus Asks

How do we answer them today?

LORI VAN WINDEN

Cover photo by Atsushi Maekawa

Scripture quotations, unless otherwise indicated, are taken from the New American Standard Bible. Other translations referenced are Amplified Bible Classic (AMP), Living Bible (TLB), New American Bible (NAB), and New Living Translation (NLT).

Anecdotal stories are true. Only names have been changed.

This book is dedicated to Kai, Luke, Koa, and Naomi, sunrays of God's goodness, each. May you live with the passion and purpose of true disciples of Jesus, and always always always know how very much you are loved.

Table of Contents

Introduction

As children, my sister and I would squeal with delight when our dad slipped the pencil off the top of his ear (he always seemed to have one perched there) and began calculating how old we were – in days. Like many other children, we were in much too great a hurry to grow up, and, from where we stood, it seemed quite impressive that I was not just seven years old, but 2,576 days! And my sister was close behind at 2,105 days. We'd strut around the room, feeling, oh, so worldly! Then we'd beg Dad to please compute our age in *hours*. As he sat with pad and pencil, we'd hover over him, watching with giggly anticipation as a gargantuan number appeared before our eyes. Then the celebratory parade would begin all over again.

Time and perspective are so relative, aren't they?

Have you ever watched a rock skip across the surf? When expertly thrown, it can seem to glide on forever as it gently kisses the waves. Often, in both the Old and New Testaments, God is referred to as "Rock," strong, solid, abiding.

Indeed, our Lord is unchanging, "the same yesterday, today, and forever" (Hebrews 13:8). Timeless. Constant. Eternal. The Rock of Ages.

So, even though we live in an earthly era different from when our Savior dwelt among us 2,000 years ago, the reigning spiritual kingdom endures: "… with the Lord one day is like a thousand years, and a thousand years like one day" (2 Peter 3:8). It may look as if everything has changed during the last two millennia but, from the vantage of eternal truth, really nothing has. It was but two days ago in God's sight that our "Rock" walked across the sea.

Thus, the questions Jesus asked then are just as pertinent today. Contexts may be different but principles are without shift. This revelation is exciting in that we can read the Gospels and ponder our Lord's inquiries with the understanding that He still communicates with us just as surely as He spoke to His disciples and followers back in the day. He continues to teach us by story and example, and challenge us with multi-dimensional questions.

While not intended to be a scholarly interpretation of Scripture, this work will conscientiously explore 40 questions Jesus asked *then* and how they are equally relevant and applicable *now*.

I pray you and I will be encouraged and energized by this study. Further, I hope our reflections here will be a springboard to new and higher strata of revelation and adventure in relationship with our Jesus.

Chapter 1

Did you not know that I had to be in My Father's house? Luke 2:49

*A call to be about our
Father's business*

South America is home to a funny little frog that grows in reverse. As a tadpole, it is significantly larger than as an adult frog. This peculiarity seems to contradict a prevailing law of nature known to most of the rest of the animal kingdom – that, with maturity, comes an increase in size.

Jesus was 12 years of age – a time of peak physical growth – when He posed our topic question to Mary and Joseph. For days His parents had been searching frantically for the lad when they came upon Him in a temple conversing with teachers. One can just imagine the confrontation, maybe not so unlike that of parents and teens today.

1

"Why have You treated us this way?" asked His mother. "Your father and I have been anxiously looking for You."

Jesus' answer confounded His parents: "Did you not know that I had to be in My Father's house ...?" The Amplified translation adds, "... and occupied about My Father's business?"

He knew where He belonged.

This young Man hungered to learn. Curious and drawn, He actively pursued the will of the Father for His life. Even though He *IS* God, we must consider that He was also a human being for a time, and so endeavored to acquire knowledge and guidance as He matured, both spiritually and physically.

There is nothing specific in Scripture about our Savior's life between the ages of 12 and 30, except that He "... kept increasing in wisdom and stature, and in favor with God and men" (Luke 2:52). Surely, He spent much time in prayer, building a foundation for a successful, guided life and ministry. It was this wisdom, this mentoring He sought so earnestly, that enabled Him to "be about His Father's business."

I believe as we advance in spiritual maturity, in our yearning to tend to our Lord's purposes, there is actually an inversion in progress. Our body length does not diminish as is the case with the frogs, but we shed that which hinders. Old ways, attitudes, or habits are ceded to the sovereignty, sagacity and supremacy of God. We cry, "More of God, less of me!" (See the longing of John the Baptist in John 3:30.)

The temple episode was a foretaste of what was to come immediately before Christ began His earthly ministry about 18 years later. It was then that He spent 40 days in the wilderness fasting and communing with God, being prepared for His pastoral assignment, indisputably one of great power and influence.

What is God's business? And where do we fit in? We must ask Him! Find out! Then make it our business! Of course, the <u>basics</u> of His "business" are the same for us all – to love. The beauty of His design is that the <u>specifics</u> are myriad and individualized according to His plan and our gifts, talents, and hearts' desires.

This question challenges us to seek God's will for our lives. Romans 12:2 teaches us to be transformed by the renewal of our minds so that we "may prove what the will of God is, that which is good and acceptable and perfect." So, the starting point for discerning God's will is a <u>renewed mind</u>. Then, Ephesians 4:22-24 explains what it is we need to do to renew our minds, to "acquire a fresh, spiritual way of thinking" (NAB). Simply, we are to lay aside the old nature (evil, envy, lust, etc.) and pick up and clothe ourselves with a new nature of holiness and goodness. It's significant that biblical translations include the terms "clothe" and "put on" when describing taking on the new disposition, symbolizing that which is continuously upon us.   Indeed, a perpetual mindset of seeking God's will, of being about His business, sheds light on distinct paths and purposes He intends for us as individuals.

For some, this might mean venturing outside of a "comfort zone" or stepping back a bit from the trappings of a modern, busy life. It seems, at times, that we run in all directions, our lives and schedules brimming with "busyness," yet how often we may sense something is missing.

Paula had a high-paying, prestigious job, but experienced a gnawing sense of dissatisfaction. When she sought the Lord, she felt directed to quit her position. What she did though, was compromise. She couldn't bring herself to completely let go, so she reduced her hours to part-time. Things in her life did not get easier. In fact, there were more turmoil and confusion than before. She finally quit her job altogether and the Lord eventually led her into a wonderful career, one she finds more rewarding and fulfilling than she could have ever imagined.

For Paula, it was a job change. For another, it might be reconciling with a friend, fostering children, or working through a difficult situation in a marriage. It may be supporting a cause, volunteering, a renewed commitment to health, more focused prayer, a lifestyle adjustment. There are endless possibilities. The point is, as our business is God's business, so is His ours.

We might liken the will of God to the eye of a hurricane. There is no more peaceful, protected, prosperous place than in the perfect will of the One Who designed us. Yes, challenges still manage to whip and whirl on every side, but we are not "caught up" in them. We experience a grace, a holy ease, to do what we are called to do. It is here we belong and can most effectively "be about our Father's business." Just like Jesus.

Prayer

Sovereign Lord, forgive me for so often "spinning my wheels" and neglecting what is important. Help me to have a heart that listens to You and is open to the promptings and the leading of the Holy Spirit. In big things and small I desire to live a life that is pleasing to You, according to Your will and the unique personality and position with which You've blessed me. I want more of You!

More scriptures to enjoy and employ

1 Corinthians 7:17; 12:4-11,18-20

Ephesians 5:17

1 Peter 4:2

Psalms 143:10

Colossians 1:9

Romans 12:6-8

Titus 2:12

John 3:30

Chapter 2

But who do you say that I am? Luke 9:20

A call to examine and share
Who He is in our lives

Snowbird. Little Brown Bear. Noisy Stream. Native Americans traditionally choose names for their children that are very descriptive, drawing on natural phenomena, personality traits, and even familial and tribal expectations. Interestingly, a child's name may be changed one or more times depending on circumstances and evolving character qualities.

The first layer of our opening question invites us to examine Who Jesus is in our lives. The Bible provides a constellation of names for Jesus, each depicting Who He can be to us if we so allow Him. Among them are: Son of God, The Good Shepherd, The Alpha and Omega, The First and The Last, Healer, Deliverer, Light, Rock, Joy, Strength, The Morning Star, The Almighty, King of Kings, The Lion of Judah, Lamb, Creator, Faithful Witness.

Meditating on each one of these individually can provide tremendous insight into the person of Jesus and, in turn, the nature of God. Surely, we can and should call God by many names. But, do you know what He calls Himself? In Exodus 3:14, John 8:28, and Mark 6:50 (AMP) He refers to Himself as, "I Am." That tells us He is the God of now, of today, of the present – not the God of regrets and mistakes of the past, nor of fears and apprehensions of the future. He is where we are now, waiting to reveal Himself in just the way we need Him at this moment.

In the sixth chapter of John's gospel (AMP), we find the disciples in a boat battling a storm. Verse 19 tells us darkness had fallen and they had rowed three or four miles, not an easy feat in rough waters. Jesus approached them, walking on the waves. Now, check out verse 21: "... they were quite willing and glad for Him to come into the boat. And now the boat went at once to the land they had steered toward. And immediately they reached the shore toward which they had been slowly making their way." Wow! The disciples weren't seeing much progress doing things their own way, but as soon as He was invited in, their struggle ended, their goal was reached. Jesus is our life Partner! He is our close Friend! In every situation and circumstance, He is Who and What we need.

Secondly, this question encourages us to take a look at how we share Jesus with others. At this point, because these two scriptures are complementary, allow me to refer back to verse 18 wherein Jesus asked, "Who do the people say that I am?" Of course, when Jesus posed this question to His disciples, they replied, "John the Baptist," "Elijah," or "one of the prophets of old." Yet, if we'll notice, Jesus hardly seemed interested in their response (probably because He already knew the answer). I suspect He wanted His friends to think about this question before asking them the one that followed on its heels: "Who do *you* say that I am?"

What a challenge rings through these words! And, let's be mindful that Jesus didn't ask, "Who do you believe that I am?" It's, "Who do you say that I am?" I find this very significant. The words we speak matter. How we share our faith counts.

When I imagine our Lord asking this question, I have to wonder what we'd tell Him. The people in our families, our workplaces, our churches and communities – do they really know Jesus? Talk about Him? Live according to His teachings?

It's strange, isn't it, that we may believe we know someone well if, for instance, we share a cubicle at work, a gym class, a carpool ride, or social media platforms. Perhaps we are aware of certain facts about them, like maybe their favorite restaurant, music genre, or where they were born or attended school, all without a hint about their faith-walk. I say that is peculiar because, like sinews hold various parts of the physical body in place and allow them to work together, so are faith and love for Jesus connectors in the Body of Christ. In the 12th chapter of 1 Corinthians, St. Paul compares the human body to the eternal Body of Christ. There is not a component that is unneeded, unimportant, or unaffected by all the rest. So, your faith-walk is important to me, as mine is to you.

A woman I know, Linda, takes every opportunity to talk about Jesus with strangers – refrigerator repair technicians, door-to-door salespeople, and even a motorist with whom she'd had a fender-bender. Once, in the parking lot of a department store, she engaged in a lengthy conversation with a homeless woman. Grasping the hands of this shabby, destitute child of God, she prayed with her and for her – in front of the whole world. Her boldness is a gift we can all hope to gain and, yes, it may have sent some scurrying away, but who knows how many seeds she's planted over the years, seeds the Holy Spirit can nurture and help grow at the right time? Linda is only concerned with doing her part.

Dear ones, we live, work, and play in the mission fields. It is irresponsible and closed-hearted for us to believe we are somehow isolated from everyone else and to go around indifferently in our happy little Christian bubbles when so many are in need of meeting Jesus. By word, by prayer, by example, by supporting churches and ministries that proclaim the Gospel, we can play a role in bringing unity to the Body of Christ. We can say with our words and our lives that Jesus is the Savior of the world and the Light in our hearts, the great "I Am." Paul shared that we are ambassadors for Christ so that God can make His appeal through us (2 Corinthians 5:20).

"Who do you say that I am?" Jesus asks. Is there someone in our life that needs to hear our answer?

Prayer

My Lord, as I invite You into the "boat" that is my life, I see You are "I Am," all that I need, the Source and Fulfillment of my heart, my Rock, my Strength, my Joy, my Help, my Way to where I need to go. Thank You for every opportunity to share Who You are. The news is too good to keep to myself! I'm sorry for the times I've hesitated to speak out because I was self-conscious or fearful, not knowing how my words would be received. Help me to understand that the way they are received by others is not my responsibility. My place is to speak out in faith and be assured You will take care of the rest.

More scriptures to enjoy and employ

2 Corinthians 4:13

Ephesians 6:19-20

Colossians 3:17

Luke 12:12; 19:37-40

Isaiah 52:6

Hosea 6:3

Chapter 3

For if you love those who love you, what reward do you have? Matthew 5:46

A call to mercy and kindness

Seas and oceans make up 71% of our earth. Huge, heaving, hungry, they are the scriptural repositories for satan (Matthew 8:28-32) and our sins (Micah 7:19). That is quite appropriate, for salt represents God's covenant (see Leviticus 2:13). In fact, when Jesus walked on water, I like to think He was demonstrating that God's mercy swallows up our sins – never to be found or even remembered by Him again – allowing us to walk triumphantly above sin, out of its control. How do we, in turn, manifest mercy and kindness?

Naturally, it is quite easy to be friendly and courteous to those who are fond of us and with whom we get along. But here, in our topic question, Jesus might be asking, how do we behave towards people who may not like us or treat us well, those who can do nothing for us, strangers on the street? When the world calls out,

11

"Ignore them," "Step on them," "Repay in kind," Jesus challenges us to do more and to be more. Showing kindness to those we might label unworthy is Christ-like.

After all, Jesus hung around people considered outcasts. He ate with characters notorious for their sin. Why? Because His mercy is bigger than any transgression and it paved for Him a path into their hearts. We can only imagine the ways in which these individuals were touched and changed by Jesus' kindness. I love this description of God's mercy found in 2 Samuel 9:3 (AMP):

- It is unfailing (it's always there and it always works).
- It is unsought (we often don't realize how much we need it or even when to ask for it).
- It is unlimited (we can never "use it up").

Freely we receive this gift and freely we are to give it.

I am often surprised by what a loving response can do, the power present in the smallest act of good will. I was in line at the post office one day, an exceptionally long and slow line. One woman in particular was fuming. She grumbled, complained, and sighed continually as she shifted her weight from one foot to the other. When she neared the front of the line, the customer directly ahead of her turned around and sweetly said, "If you are in a hurry, you may go before me." Immediately, the woman's face and demeanor softened. It was as if tension just ebbed away. "Thank you," she replied, "but that's okay." Who's to say? Maybe she simply needed the slightest bit of understanding. Heaven knows we've all been there.

In contrast, another situation comes to mind. At the local fair one year, home and garden displays lined the walkways. One display featured spas for the backyard. A very pleasant sales representative answered the questions of a young man who was inquiring about the different products available. He was pleasant, that is, until he found out this person was only curious and was not interested in purchasing a spa at that time. Without a word, the salesman rudely turned around and walked away.

We are bound to meet up with people who are not in a position to help us. It is inevitable to encounter annoying co-workers, cranky sales clerks, rude drivers, and those with ideas different from our own. And, perhaps, these times are the litmus test of the depths of our own mercy and kindness.

An incident described in Matthew 18 features a man who owed a great sum of money to his master. When he fell to his knees and begged for patience, the master forgave the entire debt. This same man, however, proceeded to hunt down a fellow worker who owed him a mere fraction of his own now-canceled obligation, took him by the throat, and demanded payment!

We will never be required to elicit the same degree of mercy God has shown us. But we are directed to model this virtue in our own circle of circumstances.

Now, let's go back to our question and look at a verse subsequent to it (5:48): "Therefore you are to be perfect even as your heavenly Father is perfect." God demonstrated the ultimate act of kindness and mercy when He sent His Son to die for us meritless sinners.

Arguably, the topmost point to consider regarding our actions and behavior is that *we are not called to imitate others – we are called to imitate God.* Remembering this is very humbling. The "What would Jesus do?" slogan so popular a while back captures the essence of the Christian heart. In any situation we need not be concerned with what our neighbor might do, or how a friend, relative, teacher, or blogger might respond. Jesus, Mercy and Compassion personified, is our role model, our standard.

And this kindness, this generosity of heart, can begin in the home. Sometimes we may feel our spouse, children, and other loved ones are testing us to the limit. How sad, though, that we can allow ourselves to be disrespectful to those nearest and dearest to us. At home, at work, or on the street, anger begets anger, tension breeds tension, harsh words spawn harsher words. But kindness and mercy invite out the best in people. A soft answer, an understanding smile, a gentle touch, an attitude of consideration can alter the course of a "bad mood in progress" and diffuse an escalating situation.

Assuredly, I'm not suggesting that we endure abusive treatment or agree with that which is unacceptable. The truth must never be compromised. What I'm offering is that we are to "speak the truth in love" as Paul wrote in Ephesians 4:15. We've many opportunities throughout the day to demonstrate the mercy of Jesus to the world.

Prayer

Merciful One, what is Your mercy but kindness to us when we don't deserve it? Assist me in showing benevolence to others even when it may seem they don't deserve it, with the assurance that You can work in these situations to reveal Yourself. How can I ever thank You enough for divine mercy? When I meditate on its scope, I see that I altogether rely on it. Thank You for sending us Your mercy in the Person of Your Son, Jesus.

<u>More scriptures to enjoy and employ</u>

Hebrews 13:1-3

James 2:1-5,13

Matthew 5:7; 12:7

1 Peter 2:12

Psalm 103:11

Proverbs 15:1; 17:14; 26:20

Luke 6:36

Isaiah 11:9

Lamentations 3:22-23

Ecclesiastes 10:4

Chapter 4

Who of you by being worried can add a single hour to his life? Matthew 6:27

A call to cast cares

When stress knocks on the door of our soul to deliver a package, do we open it wide and say, "Come on in. Make yourself at home! Let's see what you have to offer"? I think many of us do that without even fully realizing it. It's as if we believe worry is a duty or that it can change things for the better.

Actually, worry is the opposite of faith. It is entertaining thoughts of evil, fear, and dread rather than the dependable promises of God.

One of the most powerful concepts in Scripture is that of casting our cares. 1 Peter 5:7 expresses the reminder: "Cast all your anxiety on Him because He cares for you." How freeing it is when we release our worries to God, knowing He is ever ready to accept them and take care of them for us. The translation of this verse in the Amplified Bible reads like a warm cup of cocoa on a cold morning: "Casting the whole of your care (all your anxieties, all your worries, all your

16

concerns, once and for all) on Him, for He cares for you affectionately and cares about you watchfully." Ahhh ....

Some of us may be good at casting select cares, but we hold tight to others. For instance, there are those who can easily surrender financial worries to God, confident He will provide for their needs, but when it comes to their children, they can't quite let go of certain concerns. Or how about the one who can "give" his loved ones to God, but in the matters of his job or health issues, why, he wants to handle those himself! What a silly and perilous form of pride it is to imagine we are better able to take care of things than our Creator Who is all-powerful, all-loving, and all-wise!

According to Isaiah 53:4 (AMP), along with our physical sicknesses and weaknesses, Jesus has already carried our distresses and sorrows. Not only does He comprehend the mental and emotional encumbrances known to the human condition, He agonized in bearing them for our sakes. He took them on to help us, free us, to lighten our burden. Under the onus of the cross He identified them as His own. Awesome is the word for that!

To be clear, casting cares doesn't mean we sit back and do nothing, absolved of all responsibility. But, as we seek God and His direction and wisdom, we have peace. When a problem, challenge, or worrisome situation arises, we don't strain and obsess, trying to figure out what to do; we relinquish it to God with absolute confidence in Him. Ephesians 6:13 (AMP) states: "Having done all the crisis demands, ... stand firmly in your place." Our place is to pray, seek Him, and stand allegiant in what He leads us to do. His place is to fight our battles!

Good ol' Jehosaphat had multitudes of enemies coming at him. His first inclination was to be afraid, but he sought the Lord and poured the situation into His hands, casting this huge care upon Him. God led Jehosaphat and fought for him, bringing victory. This account in 2 Chronicles 20:1-30 is inspiration for the heart when we may feel like insurmountable challenges are encroaching from every side.

As an eagle soars just as easily over tall mountains as smaller, so we wholly believe God is above and mightier than whatever we may face. And since He is timeless, He had the solution to our problems before we even saw them coming. He is the Answer, the Overcomer, the Name Above Every Name.

When the Lord "knit" us together in the womb, He did not fashion our bodies to endure worry. It's not surprising that science has discovered all sorts of negative chemical reactions take place on waves of worry, anger, frustration, or feelings of helplessness. Doctors are becoming increasingly aware of the mind/body connection and how diseases and disorders often can be traced to toxic emotions. Conversely, stories abound of "terminally ill" patients who've laughed their way back to health. Joy is medicine. Worry is corrosive and pathogenic. So, casting cares is not only a spiritual directive but also a key to physical and emotional well-being. Human shoulders are not meant for the weight of the world.

Oh, but does it take practice to adjust attitudes, particularly when we've become accustomed to accepting and entertaining negative thoughts. Watch a new driver steer a car. He thinks about his every move, gripping the wheel, concentrating on the road. But soon, with practice, he steers almost effortlessly, making the continual minor adjustments needed to drive in a straight line. Similarly, when troubling ponderings come, we can learn to turn them away and replace them with favorite scriptures, hymns, and positive, purposeful thoughts. Soon it will become automatic and we will be amazed at the level of peace and joy that ensues. Like Jehosaphat, we may have "enemies" drawing near – some small, some more threatening – but what does it matter? Our God is bigger than any of them!

So, on the doors of our souls, I think it would be most appropriate to post a sign that reads: "For deliveries of doubt, despair, worry, stress, and fear, please forward to God. He handles all such packages."

Prayer

Caring Father, it is a form of pride to worry – forgive me for thinking I can handle matters my way or fret long and hard enough to figure things out. Like the wheels of a car spin and go nowhere when stuck in the mud, so disquieting thoughts reel and grind through the mind with frantic and futile exertion. Help me not to waste time and energy on stress, but to make a conscious, deliberate effort to remember You are here with outstretched hand. I bow completely to Your superior, perfect wisdom, and I trust You with my life.

More scriptures to enjoy and employ

Psalms 37:5-9

1 Samuel 17:45-47

1 Corinthians 2:16

2 Corinthians 10:4-5

Proverbs 3:8; 14:30; 15:30; 17:22

Chapter 5

Why do you look at the speck that is in your brother's eye but do not notice the log that is in your own eye?   Matthew 7:3

*A call to give up
judging others*

You have a brand new book in your hand. You are asked to go through the book and read the first line of each page. As you do so, you receive disjointed bits of information. You might make deductions and form opinions (which may be correct, incorrect, or somewhere in between) based upon the fragmented parts of the book you read, but, you'll have to admit, there's much more to the story than you know.

How true that is of those around us!

Too often we are tempted to decide that we know what's going on, who's to blame, and what should be done about it. And how subtle these perceptions may be. We may judge without even realizing it. When we see, for instance, an overweight individual, an expectant teen, someone who dresses or wears their hair in a non-conventional way, or the driver of a rickety old automobile, do we make assumptions? At the witness of a comment, decision, or reaction that seems unusual or inappropriate, when we read about someone accused of a crime or one who executed poor sense in a situation, do we find judgment creeping into our thoughts and attitudes?

This question shows us that sometimes we are so busy finding fault with others, consciously or subconsciously, assessing what is "wrong" with them, we become cynical and short-sighted, and may be missing what is right in front of us – our own flaws and shortcomings.

Carol is a woman who loves to talk about herself. She is kind-hearted but has a tendency to dominate conversations with news of her work, her family, her finances, her feelings. On and on she goes. One day she made the comment, "I can't stand selfish people." Could it be that we are more perceptive of and bothered by the very traits and behaviors in others that we might be overlooking in ourselves?

Bob was furious when he discovered an acquaintance had slipped $40 from his wallet. Even years later he referred to this person as a "thief." Yet, when Bob learned his car needed a major ($9,000) repair, he considered selling it – without disclosing this information to the new owner. In his mind he was justified in passing along this burden. After all, the car was relatively new, just past warranty, and something substantial was wrong with it. He felt cheated. Bob didn't see the log (his willingness to "steal" $9,000 from another) in his own eye, but couldn't forget the $40 speck in the eye of someone else.

Certainly, on any level and in any disguise, stealing is wrong. But, so are judgments, prejudices, grudges, and a haughty or superior attitude. Let's take a look at the passages immediately preceding our question (verses 1-2): "Do not judge so that you will not be judged. For in the way you judge, you will be judged; and by your standard of measure, it will be measured to you." How clearly formulated are these words! The judgment we confer returns to us like a boomerang. The finger with which we point turns around and points back our way.

It is good to remember that we are all made in God's image (Genesis 1:26-27), so we can choose to look for God-like qualities in others. Magnifying the kindness, patience, mercy, love, and humor we notice instead of the imperfections will allow us to look upon ourselves with more clarity and upon others with more compassion. Any "speck" we see (or think we see) can be prayed about, mindful that God is the potter. He is the One Who impels change, growth, repentance, and refinement, in His time and in His way.

After all, we haven't ever walked in another's shoes. Oh, we may have had similar experiences, but never have we encountered the exact situation with identical circumstances and conditions or the same subtleties and inner pressures as anyone else. But Jesus has. He has worn the shoes, so to speak, of us all, becoming like us in every way except sin (see Hebrews 2:17-18; 4:15). So, let's retire from the position of chief superintendent of the universe and leave others to the Lord.

When I learned how to drive, my instructor showed me that even when I had all my mirrors positioned correctly, there would still be a "blind spot." In order to see that particular area, he admonished, I would have to actually turn my head around and glance over my shoulder. This becomes especially important when a driver is about to change lanes.

It is just as unwise spiritually to make a move without examining our own blind spots. Jesus said,

"Blessed are the peacemakers" (Matthew 5:9). One way we can pursue and promote peace and enjoy a smooth journey is by asking the Lord to reveal to us our "planks," our own blind spots, and by frequently lifting others in prayer.

Prayer

God, Umpire of hearts, thank You for becoming one of us. You have a complete understanding of the human condition and of each soul, which makes You the only fair and perfect Justice. Assumptions and judgments are not my business. Being a peacemaker is my business. Lead me to pray for others with humility of heart and purity of intention.

More scriptures to enjoy and employ

Matthew 5:9; 7:1-2

Romans 2:1; 14:10-13

1 Corinthians 4:4-5; 13:12

John 8:4-7

Psalms 18:25-27

1 Samuel 16:7

Luke 6:37

Chapter 6

Would one of you hand his son a stone when he asks for a loaf? Or a poisonous snake when he asks for a fish?
Matthew 7:9-10   (NAB)

A call to prayer

Isn't it great fun to purchase a gift for someone – the perfect gift – and wrap it up, waiting eagerly for the time to present it to your friend or family member? Well, God is excited about giving to us, too. Look at verse 11: "If you then, being evil, know how to give good gifts to your children, how much more will your Father Who is in heaven give what is good to those who ask Him!" God yearns to demonstrate the depth of His love. So, in this question, He uses what is the closest comparison this world can offer, that of the love of parents for their child. Good parents want to bless their children, help them, teach them, and give them their hearts' desires. How much more so, God! With these scriptures, Jesus paints us an earthly portrait of a heavenly reality.

God is generous! He delights in providing for His children, but one of the "laws" in the spiritual realm is that we have to ask.

Why must we petition the Lord, we might wonder. Obviously, He already knows our needs, longings, and concerns.

When we reveal ourselves to God in prayers of faith, the bond between us deepens. He works through our act of confidence in Him. Many wonderful things He has waiting for us and we tap into this store and activate the channel of blessing by asking, seeking, knocking. James 4:2 declares, "... you do not have because you do not ask."

Although our topic question focuses on one component of prayer, there is much more to quality, life-affirming prayer than petition alone. Since prayer is a vital nexus in our relationship with the Lord, let's take a parenthetical look at the seven "P" properties of prayer.

1.　PRIVILEGE.　Prayer is a privilege. Approaching the throne room of grace anytime to communicate with the Creator, and praying in the name of Jesus, the Name above every name, are privileges of eternal proportion　(see Hebrews 4:16 and Philippians 2:9).

2. PURGING.　To pray effectively, we must conduct an attitude-check, making certain no anger, unforgiveness, envy, pride, and the like are present to hinder the answer.　We are to be humble and clean before the Lord.

3. PRAISE.　Prayer is jump-started by praise. Simply thanking God for His goodness and kindness, His tenderness and mercy, His past deliverance and answers, and for Who He is, not only brings joy but it stirs

up our faith by reminding us what a good and able Father we serve.

4.   PETITION.   As we lay before God our petitions, for our own needs and those of others, we know there is nothing outside of His power or His interest. With the trust of a child, we deliver to Him our appeals and supplications, great and small.

5. PERSISTENCE.   The Amplified Bible tells us to keep on asking, keep on seeking, and keep on knocking. The man in Luke 11 who was awakened time and again by a friend who wanted three loaves of bread finally got up and supplied the goods because of the knocker's persistence. Without a doubt, persistent prayer is quite different from repetitive, rote, mindless prayer. We know God hears us the first time, but continual prayer keeps fresh the link to our Source, staying our mind on the One Who is our Answer and on our own readiness to receive.

6.   PATIENCE.   We do not always notice immediate results when we pray, but patience keeps our hope and prayers afloat. Our faith can be whetted during the waiting time if we have our hearts in tune with His and remember His ways and timing are perfect.   We must also consider that our Father won't give us something before we are ready, just as an earthly parent wouldn't present a three-year-old with a dart game or a ten-year-old with a new car. We should, then, aim to be spiritually mature enough to handle that for which we pray.

7. POWER.   There is power in prayer. Prayer, based on faith in God's word and promises, and offered in the name of Jesus (John 14:13) carries the innate

ability to effect change in the pray-er, in others, and in circumstances. James 5:16 affirms, "… the effective prayer of a righteous man can accomplish much." Another prayer catalyst that brings a promise of power is unity. When believers join voices in prayer for anything, Jesus guarantees, "it shall be done for them" (Matthew 18:19-20).

So, prayer is a privilege. It obliges purging. It begins with praise. It cradles petition. It requires persistence and is sustained by patience. And it yields power.

To be sure, there is no formula for prayer. We pray from the heart, with sincere longing to know the Lord and His ways. There's a story of a little boy kneeling beside his bed and reciting the alphabet over and over. When his mom peeked into his room and inquired, "What are you doing, Sweetheart?" he replied, "I'm praying, Mommy." "Praying?" she asked. "Yeah. I wasn't sure what words to use, so I'm giving God the letters and He can make the right ones."

The lesson of this precious young lad is this: in prayer, words are not nearly as important as the desire to be close to God. We come to Him just as we are, His children looking to our Perfect Parent, growing the bond between Savior and saved.

The Psalms can be excellent models of prayer – reflection pools of the human condition wherein we see despair and hope, sadness and joy, fear, anger, and confusion, comfort, enlightenment, and growth, repentance, praise, and victory. Here, we take in spiritual nutriment and will likely find expression for whatever is in our hearts. Jesus prayed the Psalms.

As a photographer is watchful for "photo-ops," the seeking Christian heart is ever alert for the "prayer-ops" that present themselves throughout the day. Mainly, we are not to compartmentalize prayer but to partake unceasingly. Communion time with our Maker is not a dinner reservation but a never-ending feast.

"Would one of you hand his son a stone when he asks for a loaf? Or a snake when he asks for a fish?" These questions and their context show us God wants to bless us and is wonderfully able to do so. They highlight the honor it is to pray and the influence our prayers have with the Lord!

Prayer

Lord, Consummate Parent, thank You for the awesome privilege and power of prayer. Yet, all too often, it is an under-used and under-appreciated gift. Assist me in making prayer a lifestyle. How grateful I am that You always listen to my prayers and delight in blessing me. Help me with my attitude. Reveal to me any areas in my ways or in my thoughts that are not pleasing to You so that I may enhance my capacity to receive and enjoy that which Your grace births in my life.

More scriptures to enjoy and employ

Matthew 7:7-8

Ephesians 3:14-21; 6:18

John 16:24

3 John 1:2

Hebrews 4:16; 10:36

Romans 12:12

Luke 11:8

1 Timothy 2:1

Jeremiah 29:12; 33:3

Psalms 2:8; 5:3; 35:27; 66:17-20

1 Thessalonians 5:17

Chapter 7

Can you pick grapes from thorn bushes, or figs from thistles? Matthew 7:16 (NLT)

A call to examine our own fruits

Have you ever watched a shopper in the produce department of a supermarket? She might pick up a peach, turn it around and look at it from every angle, maybe smell it, squeeze it, ponder its color, freshness, and appeal. If she is satisfied with it, into the bag it goes. Good fruit!

And it all began with a seed ….

We might say that fruits are results or outcomes. If I plant an apple seed, I will get apples. If I plant a watermelon seed, I will get watermelons. If I plant seeds of kindness, I can expect a harvest of same.

Our thoughts, prayers, meditations, and attitudes are seeds and they will grow and cultivate fruit in our personalities and circumstances, our relationships, careers, and health. We continually scatter new seed, and reap harvests from seeds past sown.

The passage immediately preceding our topic question warns us to "Beware of false prophets who come disguised as harmless sheep but are really vicious wolves" (7:15 NLT). "False prophets" might refer to anyone or anything that is deceitful and bears rotten fruit – fruit such as strife, division, greed, pride, idolatry, ill-health, stress, complaining, selfishness, fear. And, even though the sheep's clothing might look harmless, it is meant to veil what lies underneath – the real fruit, exposed by the deeds.

"You will know them by their fruits," is Jesus' message to us in Matthew 7:16.

Verses 17 and 18 echo this intrinsic influence of a tree's state on its yield: "So every good tree bears good fruit, but the bad tree bears bad fruit. A good tree cannot produce bad fruit, nor can a bad tree produce good fruit."

So, as we translate this truth to ourselves we see that who we are inside is made evident by the way we live, the manner in which we treat people, and the decisions we make – these are the real deal.

Galatians 3:16 and 19 (AMP) refer to Christ as the Seed (with a capital S). In Him are all of the attributes of God, just as a natural seed contains every element of the plant which, given the right conditions, it will become.

When we accept Christ into our hearts, the seeds of a new life are born into us. These seeds, when nurtured, blossom into the fruits of the Spirit listed in Galatians 5:22-23: love, joy, peace, patience, kindness, goodness, faithfulness, gentleness, and self-control. So, in essence, we are gardens for celestial seeds.

Terry works at a busy health-care facility. One day, a patient asked for her and when she entered his room he said, "You strike me as a church-going individual. I'm new to this area; will you recommend a good church?" Now, with all of the employees at this clinic, why did he select Terry? What made her stand out? The answer is simple: her good fruits were showing! No doubt her demeanor was one of joy, patience, and love, – lasting and authentic fruit.

Seeds may be hidden – within the depths of soil or the innermost corners of hearts – but fruits, good or bad, are out there for all to see.

So, as we ponder this question Jesus asks: "Can you pick grapes from thorn bushes, or figs from prickly thistles?" let us, with humble circumspection, examine the fruits in our own lives. Are they the kind we want to bear? If not, we might be nursing the wrong sort of seed. This is not to say we are answerable for the aggregate particulars in our lives, but to remember that, although God is sovereign, He has assigned us free will and a measure of responsibility for tending the seeds He has planted within us. Look at the words of Haggai (1:7 AMP): "… consider your ways (your previous and present conduct) and how you have fared." Here is stated a direct correlation between cause and effect, investments and outcomes, seed and harvest. It is never too late to get out the pruning shears and have at that rotten fruit, nor to nourish seeds of life for a new and better yield to come.

Prayer

Jesus, Magnificent Seed, I need Your help in bearing good fruit. I don't have to look outside of myself to find peace. I don't have to look outside of myself to find faith or self-control or any of the other heavenly fruits, for You have deposited them in my spirit. My plea is that I am a place of welcome and care for these seeds, a fruitful garden, so that others around me can be fed by and drawn to the manifestation of You in me!

More scriptures to enjoy and employ

James 3:13-18

Galatians 6:7-9

2 Corinthians 9:10

Luke 6:45

Matthew 12:33-35

Titus 3:14

John 15:8

Hosea 10:12

Chapter 8

Where is your faith? Luke 8:25

A call to trust

The boat held our sleeping Jesus. St. Matthew's version of this story states He was "sleeping soundly" (8:25 NAB). Then the sky began growling and the sea, percolating. A violent storm tossed the vessel like a cork. The panicky disciples woke our Lord with words of doom: "Master, Master, we are lost."

Imagine Jesus, completely at rest, being roused by His friends who were consumed by fear and dread. Might He have wondered what all the fuss was about?

First, Jesus addressed the storm and calm ensued. Then He turned to His disciples with this admonishment: "Where is your faith?"

Time and again the disciples had heard Jesus preach. They had seen His miracles and witnessed first-hand the power in which He operated – yet they had allowed terror to rise up and overshadow what they knew to be true. The fact that our Lord would even ask this question is a wake-up call for us. How vital it is to keep in mind all the times He has shown Himself faithful and mighty in our lives – when He's rescued, delivered, healed, and made a way when we thought things looked hopeless.

This question also points out that our faith has to be PUT somewhere. It is a real, living entity that must have an object of focus. Jesus asks, "Where is your faith?" Today we reflect – is our faith in people, things, our job, money, technology, modern medicine, or comfortable circumstances? If we have directed it to these or anyone or anything other than the eternal God, we've placed it in that which is subject to change – like the weather in the above account.

The Amplified Bible defines faith in this way: "The leaning of the entire human personality on Him in absolute trust and confidence in His power, wisdom, and goodness." When we lean, we are not standing by our own strength. What better place to relinquish control than to the One Who knows all, can do all, and loves us without limit?

Looking at the adventure of David and Goliath (1 Samuel 17:32-51), we see what seems an impossible situation. David was up against a seasoned warrior of mammoth proportions. What was this young lad's response when facing this giant of a man?

First, he remembered. He remembered the way God had preserved him in the past: "The Lord Who delivered me from the paw of the lion and from the paw of the bear, He will deliver me from the hand of this Philistine" (verse 37). Next, David proclaimed the Name in Whom he had placed his trust: "You come to me with a sword, a spear, and a javelin, but I come to you in the name of the Lord of hosts" (verse 45). David put his faith in the right place – not in weapons, armor, size, or experience as Goliath had, but in the living, ever-reliable, all-powerful, never-changing Lord.

Let's rejoin the disciples in the boat. Their "giant" at that moment of testing was a fierce storm. Instead of facing it knowing the promises of God were backing them, they cowered. But how merciful is our Jesus – He helped them even when they were weak in trust. He is a gentle Teacher, never wavering in His care for us, desiring that we grow in faith but loving us right where we are.

2 Timothy 1:7 (AMP) says: "For God did not give us a spirit of timidity (of cowardice, of … fear), but He has given us a spirit of power and of love and of calm."

We are led to ask ourselves this day, what is our giant? What looks bigger to us than God's protection and love? Whatever it is, we must know it is no match for our Lord. Everything, seen and unseen, is under His dominion. Therefore, He is the only sure and logical placement for our faith.

Prayer

Trustworthy One, anyone can have "fair weather" faith, where, if the sun is shining and things are going their way, it's easy to believe in a loving, protective God. But what about the kind of faith that can withstand some adverse conditions? That faith comes only by knowing You and trusting You above anyone or anything else. You didn't promise that every day would be smooth sailing, but You did promise to be always with us. When dark clouds hover, You are our Light. When aggressive winds blow, You are our Rock. When relentless rains pelt, You are our Refuge.

More scriptures to enjoy and employ

2 Corinthians 1:9-10; 5:7

Hebrews 10:38; 11:6

Psalms 33:4; 56:3-5; 121:1-2

Chapter 9

Why did you doubt? Matthew 14:31

A call to steadfastness

Good ol' Peter. That disciple always seemed to be getting into something. Now, here he is, walking towards Jesus on the water!

One can almost hear the battle going on in Peter's mind – wanting to trust Jesus, and fully intending to (after all, it was Peter's own idea to get out of the boat!). But the doubts were whispering louder and louder: "What were you thinking?" "Look at these waves!" "You're really in trouble now!"

Obviously, Peter's faith had been in the right place when he stepped over the side of the vessel, but then he wavered. He allowed what was around him to distract him and uproot his trust and confidence. But, again, we see the mercy of God for, as Peter began to sink, "Immediately Jesus stretched out His hand and took hold of him" (verse 31).

In the previous section we discussed the importance of <u>where we put</u> our faith. It is equally important that, once we've committed it, it <u>stays put</u>, that we are steadfast in our belief, hope, trust, and confidence in the Lord.

One of the definitions of steadfast is "firmly established." In Matthew 7:24-27, Jesus speaks of building two houses, one on rock, the other on sand. When torrents of rain come and winds buffet, the house assembled on loose sand collapses. The other stands, solid and strong.

How do we go about constructing a sound bedrock of faith? First, we do not wait for a storm! We build during quiet, smooth periods – times when many may be tempted to feel self-sufficient and that they don't need God. That is precisely when we must keep feeding our faith and strengthening our foundation, readying it for seasons of challenge, hardship, and testing.

I enjoy watching my son play baseball. Often, the crowd sits behind home plate, protected by a tall, sturdy cyclone fence. When foul balls come crashing into the fence, many in the crowd will flinch. It's a natural response, a reflex action. For an instant, the ball appears to be coming straight at us. We don't have time to say to ourselves, "There's a barrier between us and the ball. It cannot hurt us." We simply react.

It seems that, most of the time, after a few balls have hit the fence, reactions are calmer and we aren't so jumpy. What's happened? The "fence" is being incorporated into our belief system. We've told ourselves over and over again that the ball is not a danger until finally that thought becomes real to us.

The same can be said for other perceived threats or uncomfortable situations. When we know ahead of time that Jesus is our Protector and that He will never abandon us, events and circumstances won't have such a rattling influence. We won't have to "talk ourselves into" a state of faith in the midst of a crisis – the belief already will be fixed and steadfast in the seedbeds of our hearts and will be able to stand up against whatever comes our way.

Among the toughest weeds to pull are those with tap roots. Typically these persistent roots drill straight and deep into the earth, often before much is even happening at the surface. The benefits to the plant, of course, are anchorage and access to water and nutrients. But my gardening friends are familiar with the tug-of-war tussles associated with trying to extract them from the ground!

With every moment we spend praying, reading Scripture, and meditating on God's goodness, we are becoming more "firmly established." We are fortifying our faith-core. Each time we turn away doubt and fear and rely on God, we vitalize our capability to be steadfast. His promises fuse into our body of beliefs.

During this episode, Peter allowed his inner dialogue and tormenting thoughts of alarm to talk him out of a victory. Suddenly, he had more faith in the storm's ability to harm him than he had in Jesus.

It is comforting to know that Christ is always here for us, just as He was for Peter. For, most likely, we can all identify with that wacky disciple in one way or another. Doubts are like the "monster" hiding under the bed of a child. The more the child thinks about it, dwells on it, projects and imagines what could happen, the bigger and more tangible that monster seems to become. But, truly, monsters, storms, or anything else do not matter because still Jesus asks, "Why did you falter?" (Read: You know Me. You've seen My faithfulness. I am here.)

Hebrews 6:19 (TLB) refers to hope in Jesus as a "strong and trustworthy anchor." What a beautiful image. Faith that goes up and down, in and out, on and off, back and forth with the shifting currents of human experience, is not dependable. In fact, it is not true faith at all.

Genuine faith, like an anchor, is bracing and ensconced, hooked up to Jesus and not about to go anywhere else!

<u>Prayer</u>

Lord, Anchor of my soul, it is comforting to know that You are always here for us, just as for Your beloved disciple. You didn't love Peter any less as You plucked him from the frothy seas, but You did ask him why he faltered. You have given us each a measure of faith, opportunity to build our faith, and reasons beyond counting for embracing that faith. So, how pleased You must be when our trust in You carries us through to triumph, when we prove ourselves to be children of steadfast faith. I want to honor this, Your heart's desire, so I ask that You, in Your gentle way, guide me. May my every thought, choice, action and reaction be an expression of faith immovable.

<u>More scriptures to enjoy and employ</u>

Psalm 112:1,6-8; 125:1

1 Corinthians 15:58

Hebrews 11:6

James 1:6

Romans 12:3

1 John 5:4

Chapter 10

Why are you thinking evil in your hearts?
Matthew 9:4

A call to holiness

A paralyzed man was brought to Jesus for healing. When some of the scribes, who were among those gathered, had negative thoughts, Scripture tells us: "Jesus was aware of what they were thinking." See how important thoughts are! Our Lord knew, even in the thick of a crowd, what these men harbored in their hearts. Now, even though the musings of these scribes were of unbelief and criticism, we can safely say anything that is not of faith is an "evil thought." Romans 14:23 (AMP) tells us, "For whatever does not originate and proceed from faith is sin."

We are called to holiness, that quality of being pure and set apart for the things of God. After all, we are dwelling places of the Holy Spirit! (1 Corinthians 3:16) Holiness involves surrendering to God our entire lives and making adjustments in mind and manner where necessary. We are enjoined to be holy as He is holy (Leviticus 19:2; 1 Peter 1:16).

Water may contain certain contaminants, most of which cannot be seen with the unaided eye, so many people choose to purchase filtration systems for their drinking water. The water looks virtually the same exiting the filter as it did going in, but pollutants, harmful substances, and unpleasant-tasting compounds have been removed. The water has been "purified."

Although our outward appearance might not betray us to others, Jesus sees straight into our hearts – He is well aware of the hidden contaminants that we've allowed to come in and remain.

Just how does our spirit become contaminated? Simply, by listening to, thinking about, and spending time on the wrong things! Gossip, crude jokes, profanity, racy books, suggestive television shows and websites, disrespectful music, and immoral movies are among what may divide loyalties and vandalize souls. And often they appear harmless enough. After all, it can seem nearly everyone participates in one way or another. But Ephesians 5:3-4 (NAB) states: "As for lewd conduct or promiscuousness or lust of any sort, let them not even be mentioned among you, your holiness forbids this. Nor should there be any obscene, silly, or suggestive talk; all that is out of place ...."

If we're not careful, repeated exposure to worldly ways can lead to gradated degrees of acceptance and, pretty soon, we may be tempted to think such vulgarities have nothing to do with our spiritual life. I mean, we go to church, we try to be good; the rest are merely side issues, right? Wrong! The state of our spirit has everything to do with how we utilize our time, energies, and thoughts. Believing such choices do not matter and that we can be immune from their effects is to be deceived. Why, it would be easier to pluck out the impurities from a pitcher of water using our fingers!

Let's consider this: if someone dropped the tiniest amount of arsenic into a glass of water, would we dare drink it? Certainly not! Why? Because that element would threaten to poison the entire quantity. Similarly, how can we be sure that watching a movie with "just a little bit" of adultery or "only a few" blasphemous words won't be as toxic to our spiritual well being?

Haggai 2:11-13 presents a sobering lesson: holiness cannot be caught or transmitted, but unholiness can. It's much like standing next to someone who is dripping with a cold. Try as he might, he is unable to "catch" our health but his symptoms likely will prompt us to keep our distance! So, while holiness is only realized through a relationship with the Lord, unholiness pervades the world around us. Thankfully, though, we are in the world, not of it (see John 17:16). We can choose not to partake of the darkness and disharmony, and to accept the world's offerings only through the filter of God's Word.

When the people brought the paralyzed man to Jesus, verse two reveals that He could see their faith. So, just as our Savior saw the negative mindset of the scribes in verse four, He also perceived the faith-filled hopes and thoughts of those carrying the afflicted man.

How much clearer can it be? God beholds our innermost purposes and intentions.

Philippians 4:8 (NAB) states: "... your thoughts should be wholly directed to all that is true, all that deserves respect, all that is honest, pure, admirable, decent, virtuous, or worthy of praise."

Coming to mind are three instances in Scripture that betoken pure, set-apart "holders" of Jesus, as our own hearts are meant to be. In the first, during our Lord's passage into the world, He occupied the virgin womb of Mary – set apart just for Him (Matthew 1:23). Later, on His way to Jerusalem (Mark 11:2), Jesus traveled on the never-before-ridden donkey – again, reserved for Him.

44

And, finally, following the crucifixion, our Savior's earthly body was laid in a newly hewn "virgin" tomb.

Yes, we reside in a world beset by sin, one that seems to have lost its equilibrium – yet we can, and indeed are expected to, live holy, set-apart lives as happily-willing holders for our Jesus. This is not to say God demands perfection in conduct – He appreciates that we are human – but I believe He does expect a heart that honors Him and truly seeks what is right and good.

Our Father knows that thoughts affect attitudes, attitudes affect choices, and choices, ultimately, affect the quality and course of lives.

Prayer

Holy Father, we, as a society, place great value on clean air, clean food, clean water, but how concerned are we with the clean state of our souls? I desire that even as I journey through this dark world, I can be a luminary. But, Lord, how I need You! Wipe me clean from past offenses and steer me to walk in holiness. It's a daily challenge – there are so many pulls in the wrong direction. Only by a constant stream of Your grace can I hope to live a life sanctified to You.

More scriptures to enjoy and employ

2 Timothy 2:21-22

Matthew 5:10; 15:17-20

Mark 7:15,20-22

1 Thessalonians 3:13; 4:3

Titus 2:14

1 Peter 1:15; 2:1

Hebrews 12:14

2 Corinthians 6:14-18; 7:1

1 Chronicles 29:17

1 Kings 8:39

Isaiah 35:8

Psalm 44:22; 96:9

John 17:16

Chapter 11

Do you believe that I am able to do this?

Matthew 9:28

A call to great expectations

Here, Jesus was chased down by two blind men who begged for his pity and mercy. Before healing them, He posed the question, "Do you believe that I am able to do this?" When they answered, "Yes, Lord," a simple two-word statement that not only acknowledged their faith in Him ("Yes"), but also Who He is ("Lord"), He touched their eyes saying, "It shall be done to you according to your faith." And their sight was restored.

Just as Jesus required a substance (water) to turn into wine at Cana, and the few fish and loaves to feed the multitudes on a mountainside near the Sea of Galilee, so He sought that profession from the blind men. Their expectant faith provided the substance of their healing. Jesus simply spoke and it was so.

Expectancy is defined, "the condition of looking forward to something, especially with eagerness." When we say a woman is expecting, we know she is not wishing for a baby, she is confidently awaiting one. So, faith has nothing to do with wishful thinking and everything to do with expectation. Expectant faith in God is confidence that He is Who He says He is, has done what He says He's done, and will do what He has promised to do.

Remember the time Jesus could perform few miracles because of the lack of faith in his hometown? (Matthew 13:58) The people there had no expectation, no faith, no confidence in Christ. So, they got exactly what they were expecting – and that wasn't much. Our faith draws the power of Jesus into this natural world, into our lives, into our circumstances. It gives Him something, the raw material, if you will, with which to work.

God is a "big enough" God, for Whom nothing is impossible. How Jesus longs for us to know that. Let's look at His reaction in Mark 9:23. In this recounting, Jesus met the father of a possessed boy. Most likely, the man was trying to be polite when he said to Jesus, "… if You can do anything, take pity on us and help us!" Note our Lord's stern reply: "'IF you can?' All things are possible to him who believes." Thankfully, the man immediately proclaimed, "I do believe. Help my unbelief!" And Jesus cast the demon out of the boy.

I don't suppose Jesus much cares for the words "if" or "maybe" when it comes to confidence in Him. Instead of praying, "Lord, if You can help …" we should boldly say, "Yes! I expect!" We must know He's ready and able. We have a good Father. His will is for health and wellness for His children. Isaiah 53:5 relays this truth: "… by His scourging we are healed." These words resound in the New Testament in 1 Peter 2:24. Clearly, He has already done it all. He's accomplished that which needed to happen for our redemption, salvation, and peace. So we need only confidently and expectantly claim what is rightfully ours. Let us not insult God's promises, Word, intentions, and precious sacrifice with faithless talk. A simple "Yes, Lord" can say it all. "Yes" to express confidence. "Lord" to proclaim Who He is to us.

Our confidence in Him greatly pleases Him and opens the way for Him to work in us and for us. We might say faith-filled expectations cooperate with the Lord to bring about answers to prayer, miracles, restorations, and blessings beyond imagining.

Psalm 33:22 (AMP) puts it this way: "Let Your mercy and loving-kindness, O Lord, be upon us in proportion to our waiting and hoping for You." In our lives Jesus is as vast as our confidence in Him, as big as we allow Him to be. Secure in that understanding, why not arise and greet each dawn with GREAT EXPECTATIONS, encouraged by this promise: "He who believes in Him shall not be put to shame or disappointed in his expectations" (Romans 9:33 AMP).

Prayer

Lord of my expectations, lead me to be bold in my confidence in You – in Your love, in Your goodness, in Your power and kingship. Your friend Thomas had the attitude, "I can see, and so I believe." How much more precious it is to You when we surrender doubt and proclaim, "I believe, and thereby I see." Help me in any areas where I lack faith. As a child excitedly anticipates the opening of a gift, guide me to see the happy possibilities of each day. Thank You for living BIG in me!

More scriptures to enjoy and employ

Psalm 5:3-4; 103:1-5

Isaiah 49:23

John 20:29

Acts 3:4-5

Romans 8:28; 10:11

Hebrews 10:35; 11:1

Micah 7:7

Hosea 12:6-7

Chapter 12

Who is My mother and who are My brothers? Matthew 12:48

*A call to know who we are in Christ
and what is our great heritage*

Television cameras surround the middle-aged man as he pores over photographs, computer files, and letters in the desperate hope of recovering bits of memory and piecing together his past. The plight of this bewildered soul airs on the news with anticipation that someone, somewhere might recognize him. The cause of his amnesia a mystery, one can only imagine how lost he must feel. What is his identity? Where does he belong? Should he trust the "strangers" who tell him they are his family?

What, exactly, does it mean to be family – to be related to someone? We usually think of a relative as a person with whom we share a *blood* connection – parent, child, sibling, cousin, etc. Or the link might be in the form of a *profession of commitment* as in the cases of marriage and adoption.

When Jesus asks, "Who is My mother and who are My brothers?" He is not coming from a place of

51

amnesia. We understand He is clarifying what it means to be of the family of God as we are drawn to His subsequent statement, "… whoever does the will of My Father Who is in heaven, he is My brother and sister and mother." To follow and obey Him, to be one with Him spiritually is to be His true brother or sister. It is apparent by His words that faith in Jesus creates a relationship far deeper and more meaningful than that between Himself and any of His "earthly" relatives. Romans 8:14 says it this way: "For all who are being led by the Spirit of God, these are sons of God."

Let's consider the cross – two pieces of wood joined together at the center. It can symbolize our familial bond with Christ – with the vertical board representing Jesus, stretching from heaven to earth and even under the earth (burial), and the horizontal board indicating those in the world previously without access (reach) to heaven.

Here, each of the two possible conditions of earthly relationships is satisfied. First, when our Lord's body was pierced with nails, thorns, and sword, His *blood* seeped inextricably into the wood of the cross. Then, the powerful words Jesus spoke before surrendering His very life for us, "This is My blood of the covenant, which is poured out for many for the forgiveness of sins" (Matthew 26:28), is a *profession of commitment.*

When we accept Jesus' sacrifice on the cross and what it means to us, we are members of God's family, covenanted together. We might say we've acquired a brand new spiritual DNA.

According to Galatians 3:29 we are the descendants of Abraham, meaning the same promises made to him under the old covenant (see Genesis 15), are ours under the new. What privileges open up to us because of our relationship with Christ!

The story comes to mind of an American couple who traveled overseas to meet and finalize the adoption of their son, a child about two years of age. They'd been wading through paperwork and red tape for months in their determination to adopt this young boy who was living in an orphanage. Even though their hearts swelled with love when they first saw him, the child was frightened and wary, reluctant to leave behind the only way of life he'd known.

But, there is a happy outcome. Because, you see, the instant that child became an official member of this family, he had access to not only their name but their inheritance: food, educational opportunities, medical care, their language and culture, and the love, interaction, playfulness, and support of a healthy family unit. And he thrived.

In many ways, this touching account mirrors the salvation story. Our Lord "came and got us." Through His sacrifice, He made us His own, beckoning us to a new and better life.

It is easy for most to understand that being part of a family ensures the benefits of that particular family belong to us. How much more so, then, when we are members of God's family! Romans 8:16-17 says, "… we are children of God, and if children, heirs also, heirs of God and fellow heirs with Christ." And Galatians 4:7 (NAB) proclaims, "You are no longer a slave but a son! And the fact that you are a son makes you an heir, by God's design." As His adopted sons and daughters, we've access and claim to all the privileges and perks of His name, His kingdom.

We must have no mistaken identity. Through our faith in His shed blood and fidelity to His will, we belong to Him. And joining His family means stepping into a realm of blessing and protection that transcends the borders of imagination. It is where we all long to be.

I conclude this chapter with these wise words of C. S. Lewis: "I find in myself a desire which no experience in this world can satisfy, the most probable explanation is that I was made for another world."

Indeed.

<u>Prayer</u>

Abba, Father! When I think that You have accepted me into Your family, how honored and grateful I feel! I am Your child! You are my Daddy! I could never earn my place here or the phenomenal blessings that are promised to Your children. It is only because Jesus made the way for me that I enjoy the prerogatives of being a child of the King. Direct me to live in a manner that shows I am connected to You in mind, heart, soul, and will!

<u>More scriptures to enjoy and employ</u>

Romans 4:16; 8:14-17; 9:8

2 Corinthians 6:18

Galatians 3:26,29; 4:1-7

Ezekiel 46:17

Ephesians 1:5; 2:19; 3:6,15

Philippians 2:9

Chapter 13

Are you able to drink the cup that I am about to drink? Matthew 20:22

*A call to reflect on Jesus' burdens
and to carry our own cross*

Thank God we don't have to endure what Jesus did. He carried all of our weaknesses, distresses, afflictions, and sins. The anguish He suffered for us (the collective troubles of billions of people over centuries of time condensed into a few horrific hours) is unimaginable. Every sin, fear, failure, disease – past, present, and future – was poured out on Him. The unearthly torment happening in His being so cruelly contorted His face that it was wrenching even to look at Him. Isaiah 52:14 tells us He was disfigured, marred beyond the appearance of any man.

Yes, He bore it all for us.

So, what might be this "cup" to which Jesus refers in this question? In Matthew 26:39 Jesus momentarily pleaded with the Father to "let this cup pass from Me" as He agonized in the garden prior to the crucifixion. We see, throughout Scripture, several other references to cup as well, among them Psalm 11:6, which says, "Upon the wicked He will rain snares; fire and brimstone and burning wind will be the portion of their cup." Psalm 16:5 proclaims, "The Lord is the portion of my inheritance and my cup," and Ezekiel 23:31 reads, "You have walked in the way of your sister; therefore I will give her cup into your hand."

I think it is fair to say that the cup, here, refers to a destiny or assignment, indeed, something that holds.

As Christians, we have destinies – our lives are holders or containers for God's purposes. Jesus' cup was the cross, the accomplishment of our redemption. Before we could have life, He had to die. Our cup, likewise, involves a type of death. In that we are beings of both flesh and spirit, we can choose to "die" to the desires of the flesh and live along the trajectory of the spirit.

Our "flesh" might be described as bodily appetites, instincts, and sensory, carnal impulses. It is concerned with what feels good, looks good, tastes good, etc., while our spirit, that part of us in communion with God, yearns for what IS good.

My aunt lives in the country and she tells the story of a dog that would come to visit. This gentle old soul (the dog, not my aunt!) made his daily rounds throughout the neighborhood, collecting treats along the way. My aunt and uncle would always have something special waiting for Buster – a bite of leftover meatloaf, a hunk of cheese, a cookie. They enjoyed his visits. One day, however, Buster showed up wearing a hand-made sign around his neck that read: "Please do not feed me." Apparently, his owners had decided Buster was feeding his flesh a bit too much!

Romans 8:5 teaches: "For those who are according to the flesh set their minds on the things of the flesh, but those who are according to the Spirit, the things of the Spirit." Romans 13:14 (NAB) implores us "… put on the Lord Jesus Christ and make no provision for the desires of the flesh." And Galatians 5:17 says: "For the flesh sets its desire against the Spirit, and the Spirit against the flesh; for these are in opposition to one another ...."

This is not to say our senses are an evil commodity. Obviously God gave them to us to navigate and enjoy our world. It is when they become lustful, excessive, consuming, and used contrary to God's ways and to the exclusion of truth that they become problematic. For instance, there is nothing wrong with taking pleasure in a piece of chocolate, but when that piece turns into 20, watch out! The flesh is in control! Likewise, God furnished us with an eye for beauty, but when this becomes twisted into a leaning towards adultery or an addiction to pornography we have, again, a skewed counterfeit of the original design.

Each time we choose something because we know it's right even though our flesh or natural impulses might beg us to do otherwise, the strength of our spirit increases and our flesh suffers and begins to die. For example, a young boy who has promised to mow a lawn for his neighbor on Saturday morning gets a last minute invitation to go to the movies with friends. Does he abandon his commitment and give in to what his flesh wants to do? Or does he honor his promise to help his neighbor?

Once, after purchasing some tickets, I was handed an extra $10 in change. I must admit, for a split second before I returned the money, my flesh reminded me of how nice it would be to keep the cash, and that nobody would ever know.

A man endeavoring to lose weight and lower his cholesterol levels might choose to eat an apple rather than a doughnut, even though his mouth waters for something gooey and sweet.

We are all familiar with the cartoons where a character is struggling to make a decision of some sort, and a miniature "devil" pops up on one shoulder and an angel on the other – both trying to convince the fellow of what he should do. He turns his head back and forth listening to one, then the other. What does he do? Whose advice does he heed?

Jesus encountered this very situation in the desert. Imagine how hungry He must have been after fasting for 40 days. It was when Jesus' earthly body was in this vulnerable state that satan came and tempted Him, saying, "If You are the Son of God, tell this stone to become bread." Jesus didn't listen. Instead, He quoted the written word back at him: "It is written, 'Man shall not live on bread alone'" (Luke 4:3-4).

Romans 8:17 says we suffer with Christ. Jesus' body, His flesh, was *literally crucified.* It was actually beaten, nailed to the cross, and it died. Our flesh is to be crucified in a *figurative* way. And the more we crucify the flesh by not giving in to it, the weaker its voice will become. When I returned the extra money, when the young boy mowed his neighbor's lawn, when the man left behind the doughnut, another nail was driven into our flesh, bringing it closer to death. Unfortunately, the converse can be true, as well. Those that routinely listen to "the devil on their shoulder" risk traversing descending paths of destruction including health and relationship woes, and proclivities to extremes (gluttony, alcoholism, pride, workaholicism, just to name a few). Worst of all, because they neglect their spirit, it begins to hush and they suffer a diminishing ability to hear God's voice.

Jesus asks, "Are you able to drink the cup that I am about to drink?" Although we can't do what He did on that Good Friday 2,000 years ago, our cross, our cup, our destiny today is to die to a sinful nature – to deprive fleshly tendencies of any leverage over us. If you stop feeding a viscous dog, he will become weaker and weaker until he eventually dies. The same can be said of our flesh. When we stop nurturing it by allowing it to dominate our thoughts, attention, and choices, it will wither and die, freeing us to the wonders of Spirit-led lives.

Prayer

God of my spirit, it is not humanly possible to thank You enough for what Jesus did for me. The cross He bore was burdensome beyond human contemplation. But I can listen to and heed Your words about my own cross: "If anyone wishes to come after me, he must deny himself, and take up his cross daily and follow Me" (Luke 9:23). So, I pray that my pursuits are always clothed in the garment of self-control and tempered by the touch of Your truth, so that my spirit is fully alive to You!

More scriptures to enjoy and employ

Romans 6:6; 7:18-25; 8:7

2 Corinthians 1:5

John 16:33

Colossians 2:9-14; 3:5

2 Timothy 2:11

Hebrews 2:9

1 Peter 2:11,19-24

Zechariah 3:1

Chapter 14

Suppose one of you has a sheep and it falls into a pit on the sabbath – will he not take hold of it and pull it out?
Matthew 12:11 (NAB)

A call to make love the
ultimate law

This question is Jesus' response to a group of "religious" folks who were hoping to hatch an accusation against Him. Ever mindful of the laws of their religion, when they saw a man with a withered hand, they seized the opportunity to ask Jesus if it were lawful to heal on the sabbath.

"Suppose one of you has a sheep and it falls into a pit on the sabbath," the Lord replied, "Will he not take hold of it and pull it out? Well, think how much more precious a human being is than a sheep. Clearly, good deeds may be performed on the sabbath." We can see exactly what our Lord did here. In short, He made love the ultimate law. He elevated the well-being of the afflicted man, a precious child of God, above the law.

The Old Testament is replete with laws and regulations, all of which served a vital purpose at that time in human history. The legislative theme of many Old Testament writings, particularly the book of Leviticus, helped the people know God and what He required to be in covenant with them.

The New Testament reveals, "In His own flesh He abolished the law with its commands and precepts" (Ephesians 2:15 NAB).

Romans 10:4 tells us Jesus is the end of the law. The Amplified version says, "The purpose of the law is fulfilled in Him." And since God is love (1 John 4:16), and Jesus is God made flesh (John 1:14), then Jesus is love! The purpose of the law is met in love!

Recently in my city, the police set up a sting of sorts at a busy intersection. An undercover officer stood at the corner "waiting" to use the crosswalk. Motorist after motorist blew on by (and received either warnings or citations up the street). Oh, occasionally a car would stop and let the officer cross, but the number of those who ignored our state's yield-to-pedestrians mandate was staggering. It's easy to speculate on the motivation of any particular driver: "I'm late for an appointment." "Someone else will stop." "I'll just hurry right on through."

But, it is also easy to imagine that, had the pedestrian been a loved one, the driver would have stopped without hesitation. Motivated by love rather than law, his thoughts might have been more along these lines: "I love this person, so what's important to him is important to me. And right now what's important to him is crossing the street safely and quickly."

If we pause and think about it, this makes perfect sense. In an ideal world where everyone genuinely loves his neighbor, there would be no cause for laws of any kind. No one would steal, cheat, lie, or have any desire for selfish gain. Those in need would receive assistance, not from government programs, but from their brothers and sisters in Christ. Each person would be trying to out-bless his neighbor because that's what Love does. That's what Love is.

Deuteronomy 6:4-5 and Leviticus 19:18 make reference to loving God and neighbor. In the New Testament (Matthew 22:37-40), Jesus says, "'You shall love the Lord your God with all your heart, and with all your soul, and with all your mind.' This is the great and foremost commandment. The second is like it, 'You shall love your neighbor as yourself.' On these two commandments depend the whole Law and the Prophets."

Jesus (Love in the flesh) didn't necessarily change the law but He brought life to it. He evidenced, by word and deed, that the law is founded on love.

You see, love is what makes things work. It makes faith work (Galatians 5:6), and it is precisely why Jesus' sacrifice was so powerful. The work of the cross was of the purest motivation of all – love.

Let's imagine parents leaving their young child in the care of a babysitter. They attach a schedule and list of instructions to the refrigerator. The babysitter could be legalistic and strictly enforce those guidelines, or she could see that her young charge is especially hungry and move dinnertime up 15 minutes, or notice he is a bit weepy about going to sleep at bedtime, and so decide to read him a story to calm him.

As we regard Jesus' question do we see that, simply by following the lead of Love, we can be assured we will always do the right thing, the Christian thing, the "lawful" thing?

The old law was but a template, written on stone by the finger of God (see Exodus 24:12). Now, not only can nothing take root in stone (Matthew 13:5), it is also rigid and unyielding. But in Jeremiah 31:33, God tells of the coming of the new covenant: "I will put My law within them and on their heart I will write it," The old was etched on hardened stone, the new on hearts of love. The linear, one-dimensional law is, at last, four-dimensional – having breadth, length, height, and depth (see Ephesians 3:18).

It comes to this: today, we should no longer need the impetus of the old written law because we have a greater law in place in our hearts.

In 1 Samuel 20:16, Jonathan made a covenant with David. In the very next verse, he made David swear again, "this time by his love for him" (TLB). Obviously, Jonathan understood love forges a more powerful commitment than a fleeting emotion. Much later, in 2 Samuel 9, we read how this covenant of love endured.

If religion is only about following a set of rules, regulations, and commandments, then it is just that, religion – stony and inflexible, yet easily broken, like the tablets on Mt. Sinai (Exodus. 32:19). But, if religion makes love the ultimate law, the impetus in our lives, suddenly it springs to life (as Jesus brought life to the law) and becomes all about our relationships with God and neighbor. It is personal and profound, prizing the ways of God and the welfare of others.

Fidelity to the law was a point of contention between Jesus and the religious authorities of His day. Unable to grasp the spirit-force of a multi-dimensional law, they were rigid as stone, ready to pounce on our Lord for violating any letter of the written law. Legitimately, a shriveled hand was not a life-threatening emergency. The healing could have waited for another day. But Love did not want to wait. Love wanted the man whole and well on that day. And Love said, "Stretch out your hand."

Prayer

Lord of Love, live in me! I don't want a stony heart; I hunger for a heart of love – like Jesus. I know this doesn't mean I blindly accept everything, there is still the light of truth and the dark of evil. But LOVE desires the best. Love prays for, hopes in, and uplifts others. The beauty of it all is that inviting love into any situation, however volatile or hopeless it may seem, guarantees Your presence is there as well. Help me to remember love is stronger and more enduring than stone. It is an unstoppable, unbreakable force. And it simply cannot fail. Thank You for sending Love to us in the Person of Your Son. Thank You for showing us what Love says, how Love acts, and Who Love is.

More scriptures to enjoy and employ

John 1:17; 5:1-9

Galatians 2:16; 3:10,13,19-25; 5:18,23; 6:2

Deuteronomy 6:4-5

Matthew 22:36-40

Mark 2:27-28

Leviticus 19:18

Hosea 6:6

Romans 3:20,31; 7:6; 8:2; 13:8-10

Luke 10:30-37

Acts 13:38-39

Ephesians 2:15

1 Timothy 1:8-9

Hebrews 7:19

Chapter 15

What man among you, if he has a hundred sheep and has lost one of them, does not leave the ninety-nine in the open pasture and go after the one which is lost until he finds it? Luke 15:4

*A call to know He is
our shepherd*

I was speaking to a woman one day who, for various reasons, recently had transferred her son out of the private high school he'd attended for two years (and from which his older sister already had graduated). She was incredulous and saddened that no one from the school had taken the time or interest to call her and inquire about this decision. Rather than feeling like her son mattered to the school as an individual, she was left with the sorry impression that his departure was of no significance to them whatsoever.

Contrast that to the scene in this question: "What man among you, if he has a hundred sheep and has lost one of them, does not leave the ninety-nine in the open pasture and go after the one which is lost until he finds it?" To Jesus, the individual is as important as the collective whole. He is not just the Savior of the world; He is the personal Savior of each human being. And, unlike a hired hand for whom tending the sheep is just a job, Jesus came for the sole purpose of making sure each sheep is delivered back to the Father, safe and sound. A genuine Shepherd, He beckons and goes out of His way to find His lost loved one, no matter the inconvenience or personal sacrifice.

In a retail sporting goods store the other day, I approached the counter to ask a question. The clerk was on the phone, clearly engaged in a personal call, and made no attempt to cut short the conversation. When she finally hung up, I asked my question. She didn't know the answer and wasn't motivated to investigate where we might find additional assistance. I'm sure the owner of the business would have cringed at the scene had he or she been there. Regrettably, her job was only a paycheck to this clerk.

We see this principle at work all around. Generally speaking, a proprietor is more inclined than would be a hired employee to run his business with concern for the customer or client, the protection of his assets, and the future success of his investment. Likewise, it is expected that the owner of a home takes better care of it than someone who may rent it. Certainly there are wonderful, dedicated employees out there and respectful, considerate renters, but, overall, with ownership comes a devotion of a higher degree.

We might say Jesus owns us for He purchased us with His blood. We are His. We belong to Him and He has a vested interest in us. He desires that none shall be lost (2 Peter 3:9). A Shepherd in the purest, most reliable sense of the word, He is concerned for the welfare and security of each sheep. If one wanders away, He will not rest until it is safely back in the fold. In fact, in the verses following our opening question, Jesus speaks of the elation of the owner when he locates his lost sheep, how he carries the animal on his shoulder in jubilation and invites friends and neighbors to rejoice and celebrate with him. What a picture!

We all sin and fall short. In the prophetic view of Christ presented in Isaiah's 53rd chapter, it is written: "All of us like sheep have gone astray, each of us has turned to his own way; but the Lord has caused the iniquity of us all to fall on Him" (verse 6).

We are compared to sheep, not exactly the most brilliant creatures on earth but I would suggest that God uses that example because sheep so obviously need a leader or they will scatter and put themselves in harm's way.

How do we wander from the safe embrace of Christ's love? Through sin. And when we stray out of the circle of protection that is God's care, the enemy (devil) will be lurking to devour (see 1 Peter 5:8). The Living Bible in Jude 1:21 tells us, "Stay always within the boundaries where God's love can reach and bless you." So, it is we who choose to traipse off and expose ourselves to danger. Yet, even when we feel lost in sin, shame, and darkness, we are just a cry of faith away. We can be certain that when we call out to Him, He will come and retrieve us.

It is interesting to note that the birth of our divine Lord was announced first to shepherds and that they very well may have been His first visitors (Luke 2:8-20). Obviously, shepherds have been bestowed an honor and a responsibility in their roles of leadership, and we are reminded to pray for heads of governments, churches, businesses, schools, and families.

Sadly, in too many of these institutions, those entrusted with authority have abused their positions and brought harm to others. They are shepherds gone astray. Thus, it is imperative we allow ourselves to be led and cared for by the one and only truly Good Shepherd – that we stay near Him, that we know the timbre of His voice.

After all, we all follow something, don't we? And if we do not choose to follow Truth, then it will be the whims of society or personal feelings, the enticements of sin, man-made theologies, the fluctuations and flows of current thought.

I heard that the best way to locate a croaking frog on a dark evening is to use triangulation as a version of surround sound. Because a frog's vocals can bounce around and be quite deceiving, it is recommended that three people take flashlights and circumscribe the general area. Each then shines a beam of light in the direction from which the noise seems to be coming. The point at which all three beams of light converge should reveal the frog's whereabouts.

It doesn't take six ears and three flashlights to locate the voice of our Shepherd. It takes but one open heart. Ultimately, we must allow ourselves to be led by Him. Psalm 23 paints a dear portrait of our Heavenly Shepherd – as our Keeper and Guide, our Source of peace, courage, and joy. This image returns in the New Testament where, in the gospel of John (10:11-18), Jesus speaks of knowing His sheep and laying down His life for us. To be sure, no one will ever love us as tenderly, as totally, as He. We are held.

Prayer

My Shepherd, You are the One I want to follow, the One Who possesses unlimited power, wisdom, and goodness. Help me to know and hearken to Your voice so that I may always stay within the security of Your care. I find it a very comforting notion that I am in the hands of an almighty, omnipresent God Who loves me enough to lay down His very life. What safer place could there ever possibly be?

More scriptures to enjoy and employ

Psalm 23; 80:1-2; 95:7

Ezekiel 34:8

Mark 6:34

Luke 15:7

John 6:39; 10:12-14

Genesis 49:24

1 Timothy 2:1-2

2 Timothy 4:17-18

Hebrews 13:5-6,20

1 Peter 2:25; 5:3-4

Chapter 16

Do you not believe that I am in the Father and the Father is in Me? John 14:10

A call to reverence the authority within us, as Jesus did

In Arlington, Virginia the guards at the Tomb of the Unknown Soldier hold to a grueling and regimented duty. With each pass, they must take exactly 21 paces across the platform, then pivot and face the tomb for 21 seconds. Also strictly ordered are personal grooming habits, uniform care, even what they can and cannot do in their private time. The reverence these guards display is palpable. They do nothing apart from the guidelines in place.

Jesus knew He did nothing apart from the Father. He walked so completely in the presence, company, and guidance of God that He could proclaim, "The words that I say to you I do not speak on My own initiative, but the Father abiding in Me does His works" (John 14:10). Jesus led a life of victory and power.

Imagine that for us − to walk so closely with the Father that He speaks, works, and acts through us − that we have power and victory at every turn! Now, you might think that could never happen for us – after all, we are not the divine Son of God. No, we are not, but let's explore some exciting revelations in Scripture.

Many believe Jesus lived in such an extraordinary manner because He is God's Son. Yet, we know He became human, facing all the temptations we do (Hebrews 4:15). Hebrews 5:7 (NLT) tells us Jesus was heard by the Father due to His reverence, not because He is the Son of God but by reason of the sincerity of His devotion, the depth of His respect, and the time He spent in worship.

That's awesome news for us. It means that we, too, can enjoy and display the good things Jesus did while here on earth. We can walk in the wisdom, guidance, and fullness of God – the One Who has a specific number not only for our steps, but also for our days and the very hairs on our heads.

Reverence is key.

God responds to reverential faith, to hearts that honor Him and are right towards Him (see 2 Chronicles 16:9). Recall the man who approached Jesus in Matthew 9:18 (NAB). Scripture tells us he did Him reverence, then proceeded to ask Jesus to bring his daughter back to life! Not a small request, this, but his reverence drew Jesus' attention and our Lord accompanied the man home and raised up his daughter.

Next, let's take a look at Jesus' words just following our opening question. Here is verse 12: "... he who believes in Me, the works that I do, he will do also; and greater works than these he will do." Wow! How could He possibly make such a bold statement? To find out, let's read on: "Because I go to the Father." Our Lord is informing us that His authority and power are easily accessible to us. He has gone to the Father and pleads and intercedes for us there (Romans 8:34,

Hebrews 7:25-26), and has sent the Holy Spirit (John 16:7,13; 14:26) to be with us.

Rudyard Kipling is credited with saying: "God couldn't be everywhere at once, so He invented mothers." The inference, of course, is that God wants us to be loved and cared for and He uses mothers as a sort of extension or outreach program.

The bad news is mothers are not perfect and even we can't be all places at the same time.

The good news: He has sent us Someone Who is, and Who can be.

When Jesus walked the earth, He healed many and taught multitudes. Yet, because at that point in time He inhabited a physical body, He could not be everywhere at once. Consequently, Jesus made the way for the Third Person of the Trinity to enter hearts, so that even after He ascended to heaven, His followers would never have to be without Him.

Our topic question imparts the news that the first two Persons of the Trinity, Jesus and the Father, are One. And just a few verses later, in 14:16 (NAB), Jesus speaks of the Third Person of the Trinity, the Paraclete. The message of the Trinity is complete with the introduction of the Holy Spirit.

According to Random House, Paraclete is translated Intercessor, Comforter, Advocate. The Amplified Bible adds Counselor, Helper, Strengthener, and Standby in its expanded definition of the Holy Spirit. And verse 14:17 refers to Him as "Spirit of Truth." So, not only do we have God's own Son making appeal for us but the very presence of God can dwell in us to comfort and strengthen, to impart counsel, to be the wellspring of Truth. And that, at last, is how Jesus could make the proclamation, "He who believes in Me, the works that I do, he will do also; and greater works than these he will do."

Now, let's turn to John 15:7 for one of the most wondrous promises in Scripture. This verse reads, as do so many in the Bible, as an hypothesis and conclusion: "If you abide in Me and My words abide in you, (then) ask whatever you wish and it will be done for you." God's word in us (and remember, Jesus is the Word and He is one with the Father, indwelling believers in the form of the Holy Spirit, according to John 14:23) constitutes the passage to a victorious, transformed life, a life of effective witness, needs met, and prayers answered.

We must reverence the Word within us.

<u>Prayer</u>

Revered One, I honor Your name – Father, Son, Holy Spirit. I honor Your presence in my life, Your words in my heart, and the authority they bestow. Thank You for Jesus, our model of right living and powerful results. Thank You that Your Holy Spirit is our "Life Coach," inspiring, teaching, helping, supporting, and ever standing by. You have provided all we need to lead lives of triumph and truth.

<u>More scriptures to enjoy and employ</u>

John 1:14; 10:30,37-38; 12:49

Mark 13:11

Luke 12:7,12

Acts 1:8

Colossians 1:27

1 Corinthians 6:19

1 John 4:4; 5:8

Job 31:4

Psalm 139:16

Chapter 17

Do you want to leave Me, too? John 6:67 (NAB)

A call to loyalty to Jesus

At a restaurant, a buffet of food stretches across the room. It is a familiar scene as, one by one, plate-toters parade by, selecting which items they would like to try. That's what is nice about a buffet. One can customize his own meal.

In John 6:26-65, during a rather long discourse, Jesus spoke of Himself as the Bread of Life. Following this address, many disciples decided to part company with Him. Perhaps what He'd verbalized was difficult for them to comprehend. Our Lord knew this would be so for He said in verses 63 and 64 (NAB): "The words I spoke to you are spirit and life. Yet among you there are some who do not believe." This is when Jesus turned to His 12 chosen apostles and asked, "Do you want to leave Me, too?"

I love Peter's response: "Lord, to whom shall we go? You have the words of eternal life. We are convinced that You are God's Holy One."

Peter's words ring with loyalty. Since he is convinced of Who Jesus is, He is willing to accept all of the Lord's teachings, easy to understand or not.

Unfortunately, like the disciples that departed, many today view Christianity as a type of buffet where one can pick and choose what to accept and what to leave behind. When a teaching or precept seems difficult, rather than praying and meditating about it, seeking guidance and truth, and making the necessary adjustments in order to implement it in their lives, they opt to "leave it on the table" and move on. This can be a dangerous practice for it places human reasoning and will above those of God. Isaiah 55:8-9 reminds us: "'For My thoughts are not your thoughts, nor are your ways My ways,' declares the Lord. 'For as the heavens are higher than the earth, so are My ways higher than your ways and My thoughts than your thoughts.'" It is a brazen and presumptuous attitude that insists God's word be molded to accommodate any particular human lifestyle or sociological folkway.

We have to know that once we truly accept Christ, convinced as was Peter that He is the Holy One, the Truth, we embrace all of Him, His every edifying word.

Not once did Jesus waver from loyalty to the Father. In all He prayed, spoke, and did, He was faithful. Thus our focus question is especially poignant as presented to His 12 closest followers: "Do you want to leave Me, too?" Imagine Him looking us – you and me – straight in the eye and asking this. Are we ready to say, "No way! I'm with You, Lord"? Many of us may think so, but our subtleties of thoughts, attitudes, and actions could indicate otherwise. For instance, who among us might say, "I would never cheat on my spouse, but I think it's okay to see an R-rated movie once in a while," or "I don't lie, but a juicy bit of gossip never hurt anyone," or "I couldn't steal, but a little creative calculation on my taxes is permitted, hey, even expected," or "It is all right to laugh at an off-color joke as long as I don't repeat it to anyone else," or "I only vote for candidates who are personable, even if they do not uphold Christian values and policies," or "I can live by most of what Jesus said, but there are a few areas where I'm not so sure – and He probably didn't mean it in exactly that way, anyhow."

My friends, that is smorgasbord Christianity. And, heaven help us, we can't customize the truth to our wants and whims. It simply is what it is. I once heard that Charlie Chaplin placed third in a Charlie Chaplin lookalike contest. Obviously, someone's notion of Mr. Chaplin differed a bit from reality, but that didn't render the actual Charlie Chaplin any less himself. Today let's not be afraid to know the real Jesus. To be sure, we each have our unique and individual perspectives, yet there is but one Truth. If we are wise, we plead with Truth to change us. We do not, indeed cannot, change Truth.

Apostle is defined, "a passionate adherent," and of course adhere means "to stick or cling to." Jesus asks, "Do you want to leave Me?" As for me, I want to be stuck, like glue, to Jesus, the Truth. How about you?

Prayer

Loyal, faithful One, You are true in all things. Your words are truth. Your ways are truth. I accept all of You – that which I understand, and even that which I yet do not, for I know Your wisdom is high above mine. Guide me to be ever loyal to You in all my thoughts, words, and actions. I want to be a passionate adherent, not to any man-made version of truth, but to You, the one and only Truth! Lord, I don't want to leave You! And I humbly pray for all of those who have – may they open their eyes and hearts to You, Who has the words of eternal life, and come running back.

More scriptures to enjoy and employ

Mark 8:34-38

2 Timothy 4:3-4,7-8

Psalm 119:151

Chapter 18

What do you seek? John 1:38

A call to focus on Jesus, our goal

Let's say someone requests that you get in your car and drive down the highway ten miles to the next town. Imagine that, upon arriving at your destination, the person asks you, "How many red cars did you see along the way?" You'd not only look at the guy as if he was nuts, but you'd have no idea the answer to his question.

Now, suppose he had told you before you left that he would be asking you that question after your drive. Why, you'd have been on the lookout, your eyes zeroed in on any and all red cars on the road. They might have seemed to even "pop" out at you.

The moral: we find what we are looking for.

John the Baptist had been preaching of the coming of the kingdom of God, of One Who ranks ahead of him, the Light of the world. So, when two of John's disciples heard him say, "Behold, the Lamb of God!" as Jesus walked by, they followed Him. Jesus turned around and asked, "What do you seek?"

"Rabbi," they answered, "Where are You staying?"

"Come, and you will see," He replied.

One of these men was Andrew, who became an apostle of Jesus.

Because of all they'd been taught, John's followers were watchful; they were primed and ready to meet Jesus.

It is interesting to note two related questions further along in John's gospel. One is pre-crucifixion and the other post-resurrection. When a squad of torch-bearing soldiers came to get Jesus in chapter 18 verses four and seven, He asked His betrayers, "Whom do you seek?" The second was posed to a sorrowful Mary Magdalene at His tomb when the resurrected Jesus inquired (in 20:15), "Whom are you seeking?"

Because our Lord asks virtually the same question several times within this Gospel, it is, for us, a reminder, even a challenge, to identify our focus.

There are two stories in the book of Numbers that welcome a look. First, consider what happened when 12 scouts went ahead of the Israelites to check out the Promised Land (chapter 13). Each of these men was a leader of an ancestral tribe, yet 10 of the 12 came back with a negative, fearful report describing the colossal size of the land's occupants. "We can't go up against them! They are stronger than we are," they lamented. "We felt like grasshoppers" (see verses 31 and 33 NLT).

They took their eyes off God's promise of protection and instead set their sights on the enormity of the Anakim people. As a result, the Israelites would wander the desert 40 years.

Secondly, do you remember the narrative of the serpent on the pole? On their journey through the wilderness, Moses' people were besieged by deadly serpents. They cried to this prophet, "Intercede with the Lord, that He may remove the serpents from us." Now, let's reflect on the Lord's direction to Moses following his prayer. He instructed him to mount a bronze serpent on a pole so that any man who'd been bitten could look upon it and live. Thus, the snake was lifted up (a symbol of Christ on the cross), and many were healed. A noteworthy point is that God didn't take away the serpents; rather, He made a new focus for His children and that focus was a way out of the trouble.

And He does that today. 1 Corinthians 10:13 promises that God always provides the way out of tests and troubles. But this declaration comes after a list of warnings including, "Do not be idolaters" (verse 7).

We can see over and over again throughout Scripture that God brings us back to our focus – Him.

> Hebrews 12:2 (NAB): "Let us keep our eyes fixed on Jesus, Who inspires and perfects our faith."

> Isaiah 26:8 (NAB): "Yes, for Your way and Your judgments, O Lord, we look to You; Your name and Your title are the desire of our souls."

If we are not resolute in our focus, in what we seek, then, like an aimless hunk of driftwood bobbing in and out of the surf, just about anything that comes along can move us, distract us, and push us around. "What are you looking for?" Jesus asks. He wants us to be keenly aware of our heart-quests.

Do we desire money? A nice home? A spouse? Healing? While there may be nothing wrong with wanting these, they should not be what we're looking for – what our hearts are set on. We are taught in Matthew 6:33 to seek first God and His kingdom, His way of doing things, and all else will be given us. So we seek not healing, but the Healer; not provision, but the Provider. In other words, as we look to our Source, everything else will be covered.

This question can be a challenge to look for Jesus in myriad places and situations: within the pages of Scripture, the smile of a stranger, the embrace of a loved one; in a laugh, a tear, a favorite song; also in a needy friend, a hungry child, a grieving co-worker; even so as we ponder the intricacies of a bird in flight, the delight of a chance meeting, the nuances of a whispering breeze, the hope seen in Spring's first daffodils poking through the soil, the reliability of the sunrise. When we genuinely are searching for Jesus, the organic Longing of our very being, we might be pleasantly surprised at all the places and ways we will find Him.

Prayer

One Whom I seek and long for, let it ever be so that You are my first and foremost Desire. I repent of having any idols in my life, any pale imitations of what I truly need, any focus other than You. In Your gentle way, nudge me along to the realization that, while I can love and enjoy the people and things of this world, none must ever have Your deserved place in my heart. Rather, I am to see You in them. Thank You that when I study the balance and beauty of nature, I am witness to Your creativity and power. Likewise, when I look at another human being and behold You in that person, how differently I am able to see him! Lord, You are everywhere. And as I continue to appreciate the marvels, mysteries, and miracles of this earthly dwelling place, I see Your hand in it all and You become more and more real to me.

More scriptures to enjoy and employ

Isaiah 26:8

Hebrews 11:27; 12:2

Deuteronomy 4:29

Romans 1:20

Psalm 16:8; 101:3; 119:37; 121:1-2; 145:5

1 Chronicles 28:9

2 Chronicles 15:2,4

Proverbs 4:25; 11:27

Chapter 19

Why are you trying to trip Me up?
Matthew 22:18 (NAB)

A call to integrity

It is good to come to Jesus when we are seeking to know Him better. I'm certain He welcomes the opportunity to teach a humble, searching heart. But here, Jesus could see the evil intent behind the question of the Pharisees when they asked Him about paying taxes. "Is it lawful to give a poll-tax to Caesar or not?" they inquired (verse 17). They confronted Him with a question designed to trap Him. But the Bible tells us: "Jesus perceived their malice." Remember, God sees right through outside demeanors to the motives of the heart.

This is a time for us to consider our own purposes. Might we go to Jesus with questions that look to justify wrong choices or behaviors? "How bad can it be?" "Why shouldn't I do this?" "Surely, God didn't mean <u>that</u> when He gave us the Ten Commandments!" Our topic question, "Why are you trying to trip Me up?" is a reminder that we can't "trip up" the truth. It's there. It's real. It's unchangeable. It can't be stretched, twisted, or otherwise manipulated, and still be the same.

Jesus is the Way, the Truth, and the Life (John 14:6). He is the same yesterday, today, and forever (Hebrews 13:8). He is unalterable Truth. It is natural for human beings to have questions, but we must be clear on whether we are looking for reasons to believe or excuses not to.

Integrity, by definition, is "the state of being whole, entire, or undiminished; in an unbroken condition." I like to say that it is being the same inside and out.

When we look at a chocolate Easter bunny, we can't tell what it's like on the inside. It may have a cream filling, or it could be hollow. Or perhaps it is solid chocolate through and through – a bunny of integrity!

The Pharisees had just voiced words of flattery even while plotting evil. Their hearts didn't match their words. They were not the same inside and out. Integrity of purpose was absent.

In a clothing store, a woman was sifting through the sweaters on a circular rack when one slipped off its hanger and fell to the floor. She glanced over her shoulder and when she realized someone was standing there, she bent over, picked up the sweater, and slipped it neatly back on the hanger. And, how about the office worker who slides a few paper clips and a company pen into his pocket to bring home? We can presume that he would not have done so had his boss been nearby. Or, consider the nursing home employee who treats patients well when family members are present, but may act differently at other times. A person of integrity does not have to be concerned about his surroundings, his moods, or who may or may not be watching because he is the same within and without. His actions are consistent with the values of his heart. Proverbs 23:7 (AMP) reminds us: "For as he thinks in his heart, so is he."

The spiritual inverse of integrity is hypocrisy. And, if we are familiar with the Bible at all, we know how Jesus feels about hypocrites!   Take the account in Matthew 24:45-51. Here, our Lord speaks of a servant who has been put in charge of a household while the master is away. If he is a dedicated worker and the master finds him hard at work upon his return, Jesus explains, he will be promoted. But, on the other hand, if the servant tells himself that his master won't be back for a long while and decides to mistreat his workers and get drunk, he will be punished and sent "off to the judgment of the hypocrites" (TLB). Jesus labels this type of person as "worthless," "evil," or "wicked" in sundry translations of the Bible. Like the hollow Easter bunny, he is only a weak shell. He holds nothing of value within.

For ourselves, do we preach honesty to our children and then lie to get out of jury duty? Or tell a co-worker what we think she wants to hear and then spout off something else behind her back?   And, upon self examination, when we may discern discrepancies and inconsistencies do we summarily shut down our faith with pitiful excuses or justifications? If so, my dear one, how we need to repent and passionately pursue coherence of our thoughts, deeds, and prayer lives, seeking God more than ever and bowing to His wisdom and enlightenment.

Remember the lesson learned from chapter 18: we'll find what it is we're looking for. If we seek and pray for integrity, that's what we will procure – a life of trusting Jesus when we understand and when we do not; a life of doing right when it's convenient and when it is not; a life of loving others when we feel like it and when we do not. Duplicity has no fit in the places of the Christian soul. As Psalm 19:14 (AMP) so beautifully expresses: "Let the words of my mouth and the meditation of my heart be acceptable in Your sight, O Lord."

Prayer

God of integrity, we can tell much about someone by the way he behaves when he believes no one is watching. Lord, help me to always remember that, no matter who else may or may not be around, Your eyes are forever on me. What freedom it is to just be the person You created me to be and not be concerned with putting on airs with certain people or acting one way in one situation and a different way in another. That's bondage! That's hypocrisy! You call us to be single-minded, single-hearted, a people of principle and purpose. If I have something ugly in my mind or heart, I believe You desire that I simply bring it before You with confession, repentance, and humility. After all, You know it's there, anyway! Nothing is hidden from You. Steer me to be the person of honor and integrity, of wholeness and consistency, that will please You.

More scriptures to enjoy and employ

Matthew 15:7-8; 23:27-28

Proverbs 28:6

Psalm 101

Romans 2:21-22

John 18:20

Ephesians 6:6

1 Corinthians 3:13; 4:5

2 Corinthians 5:12

Philippians 1:10

Jeremiah 17:10

Exodus 34:12

Luke 12:1-3

Chapter 20

Wasn't it clearly predicted by the prophets that the Messiah would have to suffer all these things before entering His time of glory? Luke 24:26 (TLB)

A call to read the Bible for understanding

"Mommy!" My very young daughter bounded up to me one day, protectively clutching a photograph of her and her brother. "I thought Grandma liked this picture." "Why, she does, Sweetheart," I replied, wondering why she would believe otherwise. "Then why, Mommy, did she say she wants to have it 'blown up'?"

Yikes! A child-like innocence had taken Grandma at her word!

As we explore this chapter's topic question, let's keep in mind that it is with unflagging certainty we can take our Father at His word.

The scene took place following the resurrection. Two of Jesus' friends were walking a seven-mile journey, discussing all that had happened. When Jesus approached and joined them on their trek, they did not recognize Him. Imagine that! Here they were talking about Him, yet failed to know Him when He walked in their midst.

After some time listening to their reasonings and ponderings, He finally said, "O foolish men and slow of heart to believe in all that the prophets have spoken! Was it not necessary for the Christ to suffer these things and to enter into His glory?" What He did next is quite interesting. He highlighted every passage of Scripture that refers to Him and interpreted it. You can bet that was quite a sermon!

Soon afterward they arrived at their destination where they broke bread. It was then the eyes of Jesus' friends were opened and they saw Him for Who He is. "Were not our hearts burning within us while He was speaking to us on the road, while He was explaining the Scriptures to us?" they exclaimed to one another (verse 32). Maybe, at that moment, they realized the importance and power of the Word. Thanks to the "stranger" on their journey, they'd been endowed with a biblical footing that enabled them to be ready to see Jesus at the right time.

And, that's the beauty of Scripture. When we so familiarize ourselves with it that it becomes internalized, we can expect appropriate, helpful, instructional, teaching verses will rise up from our hearts into our thoughts as we need them in various situations (2 Timothy 3:15-16). For instance, when we feel a symptom or ache we can say, "By His wounds I am healed" (Isaiah 53:5, 1 Peter 2:24). When an unfair accusation or attack comes at us we can boldly proclaim, "No weapon formed against me will prosper" (Isaiah 54:17). During times of sorrow we can remember the soothing words of Psalm 94:19: "When my anxious thoughts multiply within me, Your consolations delight my soul." If we are feeling weak we can take heart in Nehemiah 8:10, which assures us the Lord is our strength. Or, as successes are coming our way, 2 Corinthians 3:5 (TLB) lends perspective: "And not because we think we can do anything of lasting value by ourselves. Our only power and success comes from God."   And when it looks as if there's no way out, 1 Corinthians 10:13 (NAB) can be a source of encouragement with this message: "No test has been sent you that does not come to all men. Besides, God keeps His promise. He will not let you be tested beyond your strength. Along with the test He will give you a way out of it so that you may be able to endure it."

When we pray for wisdom and listen for God's response, it is much easier to discern His voice if we've a solid scriptural understructure. For, what He tells us and how He directs us will always be in line with His written word – never in contradiction. The dependability of the Bible is a firewall against distortion and deceit.

A friend once told me she makes her own granola so she knows what is (and isn't) in it. The same can be said for the Word. It is pure and uncontaminated. Other bodies of work, spiritual and religious writings, self-help collections, etc. may contain truths – but the Bible, from Genesis to Revelation, is the only one that IS truth.

The Word is Jesus in us. The more we read it, study it, and rejoice over it, the better we will know Him and the stronger will be His sway within us.

"In the beginning was the Word," John's Gospel starts out. That word was God. "The Word became flesh" verse 14 reads. So, Jesus is the Word. The written Word. The Word in our hearts. He walks in our midst as genuinely as He did on the road to Emmaus in Luke 24. The question for us is, do we recognize Him? Do we know He is here? Do we live by His influence?

If we want to find a recipe for chicken soup, we simply check the index of a cookbook and it will give us the exact page number. Similarly easy is looking up a website or app, a phone number, or a word in a dictionary. And, while there is a biblical answer for every human need and question, it is not usually a matter of locating an exact page number or verse and receiving very specific instructions. The Bible is not read and studied like a textbook. It is a *living* body of work (see Hebrews 4:12), responsive to each child of God.

Getting to know the Word is getting to know Someone – His character, values, strengths, and wonderful intricacies of personality. And while concordances and study guides can be very helpful in specific searches, the complete Bible is a purposive continuum of God's revelations. Its layers of complexity make it accessible to anyone regardless of age, IQ, background, or how far along he may be on his spiritual journey, so that a child can understand its messages, yet scholars devote lifetimes to its study and still cannot plumb the entirety of its depth. "Wasn't it clearly predicted by the prophets that the Messiah would have to suffer all these things before entering his time of glory?" Jesus asks. He is telling us, first, that Scripture is fulfilled through His death and resurrection. Further, He reminds us that we have every entry into discovering and adoring the character of our Lord masterfully depicted in the mural of words we call the Good Book.

Prayer

Word of God, Word of Life, thank You for Scripture, in which we behold Your face. When we need divine wisdom and guidance (which we do more often than we know!), how readily we recognize Your voice when we have in place a sound scriptural base, for You will always lead in ways which are in harmony with Your written word. Knowing Your word is knowing You! And how good it is to spend time becoming more and more acquainted with You, so that we may measure every thought, decision, attitude, and inclination with what the Bible says. Show me the best way to keep a special time each day just to be with You and to make Scripture a life-long companion.

More scriptures to enjoy and employ

John 17:26

Acts 13:27-29

Deuteronomy 17:18-20; 31:11-13

Joshua 1:8

Colossians 3:16

Isaiah 40:8

Matthew 24:35

Psalm 119:160

Chapter 21

Will you lay down your life for Me? John 13:38

*A call to give God first
place in our lives*

As Cassie Bernall got ready for school that Tuesday morning in April, 1999, we can guess she had no idea that, in a few hours, a fellow student would hold a gun to her head and ask her if she believed in God. But, that is exactly what happened to this Columbine High student, a pretty 17-year old who loved cats, snowboarding, and cheesecake.

When she responded "yes," this young woman was shot, point-blank, and killed. Cassie Bernall, a modern-day martyr, did indeed lay down her life for Christ.

When Jesus asked Peter this question, He was, in essence, repeating back what this disciple had just professed. You see, Peter was eager to follow Jesus even though our Lord had just explained to him that he could not, at this point, come with Him to where He was going.

"Lord," Peter had exclaimed in his enthusiasm, "Why can I not follow You right now? I will lay down my life for You" (verse 37).

Surely, his intentions were good but Jesus, Knower of hearts, foresaw this disciples' denial: "Truly, truly, I say to you, a rooster will not crow until you deny Me three times."

And so it went. Peter allowed fear to master him when he later denied our Lord.

As Peter's example illustrates, leading a life of victory that is pleasing to God doesn't simply spring from noble intentions. Talking the talk is one thing. Walking it out is another level altogether. 1 John 2:6 (AMP) puts it this way: "Whoever says he abides in Him ought to walk and conduct himself in the same way in which He walked and conducted Himself." Actions must match words. Of course we know Jesus did not hesitate when it came time for Him to lay down His life for us. But, can we say the same for ourselves? What does "laying down our life for Him" mean anyway?

Saints, martyrs, heroes of faith, past and present, may come to mind. Courageous men and women throughout centuries of church history, some we know about, and many we don't, have been persecuted, beaten, and killed for holding fast to their beliefs. Most of us today, however, are not presented with such extreme faith tests. Rather, we are called to lay down our lives for God in small, everyday ways. I believe this is accomplished by putting God before all else. Do we live by His word? Are we faithful and obedient consistently and not just when it's easy and convenient? Do we put others' needs ahead of our own? Do we make good use of the gifts and talents our Creator has provided?

There is an interesting story in the 25th chapter of Matthew's gospel. It is about the man who entrusts different numbers of silver pieces to each of three servants. When he returns from his trip he is satisfied with the two who have been industrious with the money, using it to earn more for their master. However, the servant who simply has buried the silver to protect it arouses anger from his employer who calls him "lazy," among other things.

Sometimes it may seem easier to bury the gifts God has given us rather than look for places to use them and to glorify Him with them. Do we sing? Bake? Are we blessed with a knack for uplifting conversation to cheer others? Are we good at organizing? Fundraising? Do we feel called to intercessory prayer? To teach the Gospel to children? To become foster parents? When we make time to pursue service to others and set aside distractions and selfish desires, we are, indeed, laying down our lives for Christ. We are walking the walk of a Christian.

The Word declares, "seek His kingdom, and these things shall be supplied to you also" (Luke 12:31 AMP). He is the Source of all we could ever need or desire. But He must be our priority, not Someone we pray to occasionally, think about from time to time, and try to serve when it suits us. And that, ultimately, is how we can tell what or who is first place in our lives – by where our thoughts and attention are, by what our actions reveal.

Most Bible scholars agree that Jesus spent about 33 years on earth, the first 30 in preparation for His public ministry and the final three walking out that sacred assignment, culminating in the crucifixion and, finally, the resurrection.

In Luke 9:23 Jesus says we must take up our cross each day and follow Him. Following Him obviously implies that He is first – that He goes ahead of us. The other day my husband and I trudged through an open field where the lush green grass was knee-deep. He walked ahead and I in his trail. I appreciated that he was "doing the dirty work," so to speak, for when he came to a boggy spot or uneven ground, I knew about it before I got there and could be prepared. One could say I was "safe" in his footsteps.

When we allow Christ to be "front and center" (and we are not off hewing our own trails which lead nowhere), our every step is guided by Him, our lives truly belong to Him.

"Will lay down you life for Me?" Jesus asks. We are expected to lay down our lives by living wholly devoted to the One Who has given us breath by making certain He is always first. And, without question, the centrality of Christ in the domain of our day-to-day worlds defines true discipleship. How our Father must celebrate when we awaken every morning with Him on our mind and pray, "Lord, how can I serve You today? How can I delight Your heart? My life is Yours!"

Prayer

Lamb of the Sacrifice, I'm sure You didn't "feel" like enduring the torture of the cross, but You did it anyway, laying down Your life for humankind. Now, I ask for strength in laying aside my willfulness so I may take on Your purposes. Let me not be mastered by the mercurial pendulum of emotion but help me to talk the talk and walk the walk of a devoted follower. My life belongs to You, yet wrung from this surrender is the way to greatest joy.

More scriptures to enjoy and employ

Matthew 5:8; 6:33

Romans 12:1

John 15:13

Chapter 22

So you could not keep watch with Me for one hour? Matthew 26:40

A call to commitment

Imagine Jesus agonizing in Gethsemane. He was praying, fully aware of what loomed ahead of Him. So much torment pulsed through His body and soul that He actually began sweating blood. When He returned to His disciples, He found them fast asleep. Jesus was about to face the most horrific experience of all time and eternity and perhaps He sought human comfort, shared prayer. Yet, He was met with the ugly stench of abandonment. His closest friends had emotionally deserted Him. So, He awakened the slumbering disciples with the question, "You could not keep watch with Me for one hour?" Then He departed to continue in prayer. Upon His return, He again witnessed the torpor of his companions. A third time Jesus withdrew and a third time He came back to a pack of men who "could not keep their eyes open" (verse 43 NLT).

Ugh! I don't know about you, but when I think about this how I long to soothe our Lord. How isolated

He must have felt. How alone. But, while you and I are not in the garden with Him we <u>are</u> called to relationship, and that relationship implies commitment today. He has proved His commitment to us. How committed are we to Him?

Since commitment is defined, "the state of being bound … to a course of action or to another person," let's consider that notion of being bound.

When two people commit themselves together in marriage, for instance, their lives become integrated on every level – spiritual, emotional, physical, financial. What's important to one is important to the other. They are a team, committed "for better or for worse," for Garden of Eden times and Garden of Gethsemane times.

When we commit ourselves to Christ, and we do this by acknowledging He is the Son of God, our Savior, and by surrendering the whole of our lives to His designs, we become bound to Him. But, just what does this entail on a day-to-day basis? We can ask ourselves, do we spend time listening to Him, reading His Word, meditating on His message, praising, praying? Or, are we lazy and heavy-eyed, tempted to abandon all serious attempts to nurture our relationship with Him? It's quite significant, to be sure, that Jesus came back not once but <u>three</u> times to the disheartening sight of apathy. Maybe this was a taste of Peter's three-pronged denial soon to come.

Daniel displayed a stalwart, in-your-face commitment to God in this verse from chapter six of the Old Testament book named for him: "Now when Daniel knew that the document (banning prayer) was signed, he entered his house … windows open toward Jerusalem and he continued kneeling on his knees three times a day, praying and giving thanks before his God, as he had been doing previously." Not concerned with who might be watching or listening, Daniel prayed. The rest of that chapter frames one of the most gripping stories in all of Scripture (more on this follows in our next chapter).

We can see clearly by the nature of our opening question how critical it is to give God <u>time</u>, and this with the understanding that we are not doing Him a favor by "making room" for Him in our lives but that He IS our life. It may be easy to offer up a quick prayer, write out a check to charity, and spend an hour once a week in church, all good, absolutely, but how meaningful it must be to Him when we find a quiet time and place just to be with Him: "Lord, here I am. I'm thinking of You. I'm with You. What would You have me know or do? Who around me is in a garden of pain?" This intimate communication fosters another dimension of commitment, and that one to God's dwelling place on earth – our brothers and sisters. You see, when we ask ourselves if we are "there" for God, by extension, we must ask, are we "there" for others? In Matthew 25:40 Jesus states, "Truly I say to you, to the extent that you did it (clothing, feeding, welcoming, comforting, etc.), to one of these brothers of Mine, even the least of them, you did it for Me."

How many times might we have missed an opportunity to offer solace, consolation, encouragement, or prayer, where it was desperately needed? No, we are not in the garden with Him, but we are here amidst many who suffer, agonize, and despair – people who are experiencing the darkness of their own Gethsemane.

A few years ago Jill was going through such a Gethsemane time. Bulldozed by her husband's unfaithfulness and a resulting separation, the substance abuse problem of one of her children, and serious health issues of her own, this once highly motivated woman seemed barely able to function. Many of her "friends" stopped calling. Perhaps they didn't know what to say or how to respond to her tears. Maybe they were simply afraid of the level of her pain. Though most certainly not their intention, their abandonment compounded Jill's loneliness and depression. A couple friends, however, stood by her through this season of intense trial, setting aside time and their own discomfort to provide what was needed – a listening ear, encouragement, and someone to drive her to medical appointments as Jill struggled to regain some traction. As humans, it may seem much easier to just walk away from such situations and pretend they don't exist. The disciples' sleep may have been such an escape, a way of not becoming uncomfortably close to Jesus' pain. But that is not the Lord's way. Jesus is not afraid of or put off by human distress. He is there with all who suffer, and guess what! Since He resides in us, that means we are, too!

In Exodus 17:8-13 Moses' people found themselves under attack. As this leader held high the staff of God, Israel made progress in the battle. When he rested, the enemy began to prevail. Aaron and Hur saw a need and stepped in to help. Each buoyed up one of Moses' arms so the staff could remain elevated all day until victory was assured. In Acts 14:19-20 (AMP) the apostle Paul was stoned and left for dead by a group of Jews. We read, "The disciples formed a circle around him, and he got up." Without delay their fallen comrade became the center of the disciples' attention and concern. Friends, we sojourn together. Along this pilgrimage do we pause to offer support for another who is worn or weary?

Psalm 34:19 (NAB) says, "The Lord is close to the brokenhearted, and those who are crushed in spirit He saves." Ultimately, we honor our commitment to Jesus by recognizing critical moments or Gethsemane seasons in others, and responding accordingly. That is precisely why this episode in the garden is so revealing and our Lord's question so very pointed: "So you could not keep watch with Me for one hour?" He is telling us, "Pray! Be with Me! And look around you and see the needs of others!"

2 Corinthians 1:4 (NLT) nicely encapsulates this ideal: "He comforts us in all our troubles so that we can comfort others. When they are troubled, we will be able to give them the same comfort God has given us."

Prayer

Lord of commitment and comfort, I can imagine how different it all could have been during Your dismal hours in the garden on the eve of Good Friday. I can imagine Your disciples praying with You, encouraging You, wrapping You and Your needs fully in their attention. I'm so sorry they failed You at that moment, I'm sorry for how alone You were, and I'm sorry for my part in Your agony. Lord, You never walk away from us but You do, at times, watch Your people walk away from You. I long for quality, communing time with You on a regular basis. Further, I desire to be a channel of Your graces, receiving comfort from You and letting it flow from me into the needs and situations of others. Help me to know that true commitment endures despite the degree of difficulty or inconvenience.

More scriptures to enjoy and employ

Galatians 6:2

2 Timothy 2:13

Romans 1:4-12

1 Thessalonians 4:18

Daniel 5:12

Chapter 23

Do you think that I cannot appeal to My Father, and He will at once put at My disposal more than 12 legions of angels?

Matthew 26:53

A call to understand heaven's powers are available to us

Twelve legion is equal to 72,000 – now that's an army of angels! But, at this pivotal moment in history, Jesus did not call. The good news for us is that He allowed Himself to be arrested and taken away to trudge the path of the cross. And more good news is revealed in this scripture, and that is the great ministry of heavenly angels.

The idea of angels has become so secularized today that it may be easy to misunderstand what they are all about. Winged, white-robed, human-looking angels float through advertisements, books, movies, television shows, and song lyrics. They show up on bumper stickers and in our vernacular (i.e. "you're an angel"). They are a safe, non-threatening reference to religion in a world often averse to all things Christian.

Yet, while they may take on human likeness at times, angels are not people transformed. Those entering heaven's gates do not stand in line waiting for the doling out of feathery wings and polished halos. Nor are angels random goody-goodies drifting around on clouds granting wishes and playing harps. Created by the Almighty, they are <u>purposeful</u> and <u>powerful</u> entities.

Their <u>purpose</u> comes from God and that purpose includes praising Him (Isaiah 6:1-3, Revelation 4:7-11), fighting spiritual battles (Revelation 20:1-3, Daniel 10:13), acting as messengers (just within the first two chapters of Luke's Gospel, angels appeared to each Zechariah, Mary, and the shepherds), and helping and serving us, those inheriting salvation (Hebrews 1:14).

Their <u>power</u> to help us comes from us. "Now, wait just a minute!" you might say, "How can we empower angels?" Very simply, by our words. Let's look at Psalm 103:20: "Bless the Lord, you His angels, mighty in strength, who perform His word, obeying the voice of His word." God created angels to respond to His word, to the velocity of spoken faith. They are at the ready, waiting for faith-filled words so they can act.

Consider Shadrach, Meshach, and Abednego, who refused to worship the golden statue set up by King Nebuchadnezzar. They vocalized their faith and were rescued from the fiery furnace by an angel. (You can read about this in the third chapter of Daniel.) Three chapters later we see another grand story of deliverance. We'll recall that even after a royal decree forbidding petition to God, Daniel persisted in prayer and in offering thanks near an open window for all to witness. As punishment, he was ordered cast into a den of lions. After a night spent sealed in a pit with these ferocious beasts, this prophet emerged, untouched, proclaiming: "My God sent His angel and shut the lions' mouths and they have not harmed me."

Faith-rich speech provides the angels with an open door and permission to do what they know so well to do. Words are troops, of sorts, that these heavenly beings can mobilize and launch into our situations.

An angel told Daniel, "Fear not ... for from the first day that you set your mind and heart to understand and to humble yourself before your God, your words were heard and I have come as a consequence of and in response to your words" (Daniel 10:12 AMP).

One of the most amazing angel stories in Scripture occurs in the 12th chapter of Acts. Double chained and flanked by soldiers, Peter found himself detained in prison. Additionally, sentries guarded the outside door. Verse 5 tells us, "prayer for him was being made fervently by the church to God." The night before his trial, as Peter slept, an angel appeared in his cell and awakened him. The chains fell off Peter and he followed the angel right past the guards to the city gate, which opened "by itself." What a moment of deliverance. We can imagine that the faith-filled words of his fellow believers as they prayed were immensely powerful.

Sometimes, inexplicable events today are attributed to the intervention of angelic beings. Take the missionary who traveled to the South Pacific. He and his wife were confronted by hostile natives who intended to kill them by setting fire to their house. The couple prayed all night and was awe-struck to see the natives leave come morning. Many months later the chief of this tribe became a Christian and, when asked why he and his men didn't burn down the house that night, described seeing hundreds of sworded men in "shining garments" encircling the missionaries' station.

A Nebraska family was vacationing in a national park when their 6-year old daughter became ill with vomiting and seizures. They drove toward the nearest town, some 10 miles away, praying they would find help quickly. They spotted a hospital sign, and then four more, which led them directly to the emergency room. After the young girl was stabilized, her mother expressed to the doctor how grateful she was for the hospital signs along the way. "What signs?" he inquired. Sure enough, when the family went back to look, the signs were gone.

Jesus knew, even as He was led away to the cross, that angels exist to help, serve, defend, and protect in this world cratered by sin. That's good for us to know, as well, yet, isn't it unnerving to think that, in like fashion, we have power to tie their hands with foolhardy prattle?

We must remember angels are not God. They are not to be worshipped, but these heavenly sponsors, if you will, are sent by God to intervene for us as spiritual warfare rages and roils just beyond the compass of our natural senses.

Prayer

God, my Protector, how beautiful it is that the powers of heaven stand at the ready, to help and serve Your children. Thank You for protecting us from seen and unseen dangers. Direct me to do my part by making sure my words are faithful, not fearful − cooperative, not contrary, so that I can avail myself of heaven's help daily, hourly, minutely.

More Scriptures to enjoy and employ

Psalm 34:7-8; 91:11-12

Ezekiel 1

Hebrews 1:6-7; 2:5-7; 13:2

Exodus 23:20-23

1 Kings 19:3-8

Genesis 19:12-29; 24:7

Colossians 2:18

John 1:51

1 Peter 5:8

2 Corinthians 10:4

Revelation 22:8-9

Ephesians 6:12

Romans 8:38

Matthew 18:10; 25:31

Luke 12:8; 15:10; 22:43

1 Corinthians 6:3

Chapter 24

Do you want to be healed? John 5:6 (NAB)

A call to embrace the fullness
of the salvation package

Sheila wanted to buy a puzzle as a gift for her friend. As she entered the store, one puzzle immediately caught her eye. The front of the box depicted a beautiful vineyard scene with hovering hot air balloons and a glorious backdrop of mountains. "This is it," she thought as she picked up the box marked "500 pieces."

"Just to let you know," the clerk told her as she rang up the purchase, "this puzzle is missing 50 pieces."

"What?!" asked Sheila incredulously. "Then I do not want it!"

"Suit yourself," said the clerk with a hint of indignation, "but you know there are 450 perfectly good pieces in there."

Of course we never would expect such an exchange to actually happen yet it helps illustrate just how pointless is an incomplete gift.

God wants us whole in every area. He wants our bodies well and healthy, our emotions balanced, our relationships with Him and with family and friends to be intact and peaceful, and our finances, stable.

We must refuse to settle for brokenness in any form. Accepting anything less than wholeness is to insult the very sacrifice of Jesus Christ. Now, that may sound like a radical statement, but the salvation He came to give is not a partial or temporary accomplishment as were the animal and grain sacrifices of the Old Testament.

Although very few Christians would dare say Jesus cannot heal, a surprising number believe He won't or might choose not to. Yet, no Christian would deny that Jesus came to earth, died, and rose to bring us salvation. That is Christianity 101. So, we are beckoned to take a deeper look into the inclusiveness of this gift.

Thankfully, and to God's glory, salvation involves more than just the forgiveness of sins and going to heaven. In the book of Acts (chapter four, verse 10 NAB), in reference to an individual who had been born crippled, Peter said, "In the power of that Name this man stands before you *perfectly sound.*" In verse 12 he continues: "There is no *salvation* in anyone else." "Perfectly sound" and "salvation" were both translated from the same Greek word that means "to make whole." One of the Hebrew words translated to salvation is defined, "prosperity, welfare, deliverance, victory." So, our working definition of salvation can be "wholeness, completeness, well-being."

Jesus' words in John 10:10 (AMP) back this up as He declares, "I came that they may have and enjoy life and have it in abundance, to the full, till it overflows."

Too many remain stuck in stale traditions and antiquated ways of thought which would have us believe God wants us to be sick and oppressed or that He sends disease, poverty, and hard times our way to teach us lessons.

Yes, we live in a fallen world. Yes, there is suffering and misery. But that is not God's will for us. If we consider the original paradise He created for His children, we will know that it was perfect and beautiful.

Let's return to the scene in John 5. This man had been ill 38 years. When Jesus asked him, "Do you want to be healed?" He waited to hear the man's own words, his affirmation, his will lining up with God's. Notice what this man answered – He replied to a potentially life-changing, freeing, restorative inquiry with a "but," a note of hesitancy. "I have no man to put me into the pool when the water is stirred up, but while I am coming, another steps down before me" (verse 7). He was looking at the limitations of the physical world. How often might we reason ourselves right out of God's will of healing by considering conditions in the natural realm?

I love Jesus' response. He was not about to give those doubts and concerns of the sick man a second thought. "Get up, pick up your pallet and walk!" He commanded the man to take a step of faith.

Throughout the New Testament we find that Jesus never turned away anyone who asked for healing. God received glory when people were made whole (Luke 5:25-26; 7:16-17). Time and again our Lord said, "I do will it – be healed." If He willed it then, He wills it today for in Him is no shadow of change (James 1:17). Let's tell Him, "Yes! I want it! Jesus, I know You died for me, bearing all my burdens. Why should I carry them again? I receive all You have done for me."

Worth noting at this point is verse 14 of John 5 (NAB) where our Lord encountered the healed man later in the temple precincts. This is what He said to him: "Remember, now, you have been cured. Give up your sins so that something worse may not overtake you." Here is a reminder that there is evil in the world, and a warning that it looks for opportunities to slither in just as it did in the Garden of Eden. Eden was spotless, pristine, and in every way good until sin was invited in through man's disobedience – then darkness and evil were unleashed upon it. Do we see? That is why it was necessary for Jesus, Himself spotless, pristine, and in every way good, to come and restore our standing with the Father. He not only took on the sin that had overrun the garden, but the effects of that sin, as well – disease, distress, paucity, and the gloom and frenzy of a fractured world. He did that for us! "He made Him Who knew no sin to be sin on our behalf, so that we might become the righteousness of God in Him," proclaims 2 Corinthians 5:21. Here, before us, is the cosmic paradox of Christianity. Jesus' assumption of human sin became our passageway to holiness: His death to our life; His nails to our freedom; His brokenness to our wholeness – all together, His beauty for our ashes.

When we face a need for healing in any area – physical, emotional, spiritual, in relationships, attitudes, or finances, we must first know that God wants us whole (see Isaiah 53:5 and 1 Peter 2:24) and that Jesus died to render all things possible. Additionally, though, our behaviors should be cooperative in all of this. Taking good care of our bodies, mitigating stress, making prudent financial decisions, and practicing kindness, for instance, all work in concert with the Creator's original paradigm.

Just as the Garden of Eden contained the power and promise of the kingdom before sin was introduced, so we must be sinless to enjoy the fullness of the salvation package. And, most assuredly, we cannot do that on our own. We need God's help and direction at every turn, and to repent immediately when we've missed the mark, made a wrong choice, or caused an offense. The redemptive blood of Jesus is our only hope. Happily,

Father God sees us, His children, through the blood of His Son.

Psalm 35:27 tells us God wills the prosperity of His servants – some translations use the wording, "He delights" or "takes pleasure in" the prosperity of His children. Let us accept, without doubt, dispute, or dilution, the Father's perfect intentions toward us. Then we can confidently claim what is rightfully ours as Christians: wholeness.

Prayer

Saving Lord, You so desire Your people's wellness, wholeness, happiness, and health that You allowed Your only Son to be sacrificed to return Eden to planet Earth. I will to keep the garden of my soul clean, a welcoming home for You. I dare to believe You are so good and so loving, that it delights Your heart when we align our wills with Yours, stand on Your promises, and accept this gift of salvation in its entirety. Guide our thoughts, reveal in us places that are broken, areas in need of restoration. Jesus come in and heal!

More scriptures to enjoy and employ

Psalm 103:3; 116:8

Matthew 7:9-11; 8:16-17

Jeremiah 29:11

Mark 9:14-27

Romans 4:19-21

Deuteronomy 30:19

Proverbs 4:20-23

Exodus 23:25-26

Hebrews 9:12

Isaiah 61:3

Chapter 25

How can you, being evil, speak what is good? Matthew 12:34 (AMP)

*A call to know the
power of words*

Have you seen the baked bean commercials with the speaking dog? Or the sarcastic feline in the cat food advertisements? Remember Mr. Ed, the talking horse? Producers have a fanciful time with the notion of animals endued with the gift of gab. But, isn't it significant that human beings are the only creatures who have words and the apparatus of organized language? Sure, animals communicate through sounds, chemicals, motions, and the like, but we alone have the privilege – and the responsibility – of having at our disposal precise and powerful words.

Words are, indeed, packages of power – of highly consequential spiritual power. Prophetic in our lives, they can build up or tear down. And they are God's modus operandi.

God Himself <u>spoke</u> the heavens and all of creation into existence. God said, "Let there be light" and there was light. Then He said, "Let there be an expanse in the midst of the waters," and so it happened (see Genesis 1:3,6). And thus it goes throughout the account of creation; God said and it was. That's what Romans 4:17 describes as calling into being that which does not exist.

Now, you may be thinking, "Certainly the words of a human aren't full of any great power." They are if they are filled with faith! We are made in God's image. And Jesus is our example. He never spoke idle, purposeless words – only words of faith. When He said, "Quiet! Be still!" to the storm, His words had effect. When He commanded the sick to be healed, His words produced results. And He told us we can do the same thing (Mark 11:23).

When we face problems, challenges, and obstacles, Jesus doesn't recommend we wish them away or cry and complain until they disappear. He instructs us to boldly <u>speak</u> to those mountains. When Mary, the mother of our Lord, was told she'd been chosen to bear the Son of God, she confirmed this assignment and opened the way for the Holy Spirit to work with these words of faith: "I am the servant of the Lord. Let it be done to me as you say" (Luke 1:38 NAB). There are many other examples in the Bible of faith-activating words. In 1 Samuel 17:36,37,45-47, the story of David and Goliath, young David spoke resolute, courageous words before killing this Philistine. We also recall the narrative of Talitha in Mark 5 where Jesus put out of the room those who didn't believe beyond what their senses could tell them, before raising up this young girl. We've discussed in previous sections how angels respond to faith-laden words and how Jesus Himself often would call for verbal professions of faith from the sick before He healed them.

Faith is taxied on words. It enters the heart that way (Romans 10:17), and it is released the same way (2

Corinthians 4:13). But, faith can be in the wrong place. Faith in the power of sickness, calamity, inflation or any other destructive force can bring reciprocal power. That's why Proverbs 18:21 tells us the power of life and death is in the tongue. James 3:6 (NAB) refers to the tongue as a "universe of malice." People who say, "I get the flu every year" get the flu every year. Those who lament, "My kids are always in trouble" have kids who are always in trouble. That's the faith in their hearts, and their words continually catalyze it.

I remember a riveting testimony on television by a woman who had developed a chronic fever. Exhaustive medical testing failed to uncover its source. Doctors were baffled, but the fever raged on week after week, month after month. Finally, it was revealed to her that she had developed a habit. The woman had not realized how frequently and almost subconsciously she'd been uttering the phrase, "That burns me up" to express anger or irritation. When she repented of these frivolous words and stopped using them, the fever went away.

Individuals who repeat as mantras phrases such as, "I'm getting so forgetful," "I'm always late," "I keep gaining weight," "My blood pressure is out of control," "I never have enough time to get everything done," or "I can't afford it," don't realize they are prophesying negativity into their futures. The angels of heaven can't use these words but the forces of evil salivate at the prospect of securing a foothold in them.

I like this statement of David in response to those out for his ruin: "But I, like a deaf man, do not hear; and I am like a mute man who does not open his mouth" (Psalm 38:13). He knew it is better to keep silent than to crank out words of fear or frustration. Jesus warns we are accountable for every unguarded word we speak (Matthew 12:36).

Words, like cobbles on a walkway, must lead somewhere. Indeed the TYPE of words issued forth from the mouth determines if it is good faith or bad faith that is loosed – whether these verbal cobbles contour a path to God's intended will or pave a trail toward defeat.

Of course, it takes practice and grace to break the habit of negative talk. Let's go back to our opening question: "How can you, being evil, speak what is good?" We see the key to positive confession is watching over what is in our hearts. What we allow to saturate our hearts will spill out into our words, which, in turn, have a defining effect on our lives. Just two verses later (36 and 37), Jesus said, "every careless word that people speak, they shall give an accounting for it in the day of judgment. For by your words you will be justified, and by your words you will be condemned."

When someone comes at us with an ominous report, we can respond with words reflecting the faith in our hearts. For instance, we may hear: "There are going to be lay-offs at your place of employment." We can say: "I know God has a good plan for my life. I have favor." Or we might hear: "The flu is going around" to which we can respond, "God is my shield. I am strong and healthy." Or we may encounter a comment such as, "The Smiths are headed for divorce." An appropriate reply can be, "I will pray for peace and healing in that family." We can choose to avoid being caught up in faithless bramble.

In the final chapter of the book of Joel, this prophet proclaimed, "Let the weak SAY 'I am strong (a warrior)'" (verse 10 AMP). Because Jesus, the Light of the World, the WORD made flesh, resides in us, we can always be ready with a positive profession. In fact, He IS the High Priest of our confession (see Hebrews 4:14).

To a great degree, we are the architects of our destinies – our faith is the blueprint and our words are the bricks, stones, and planks that help frame our futures. And, like any strong building, words endure. I'm sure each of us can recall a particular something someone has said to us in the past, maybe a word of hope, perhaps a comment of hurt. Words, even those released decades ago, can echo in our minds. I once read that if we only had the technology, we could retrieve actual speech voiced centuries ago. Imagine listening to such American greats as Abraham Lincoln or Benjamin Franklin. How about tuning in to the articulations of Joan of Arc or William Shakespeare? Once uttered, words ricochet through time and space, everlastingly "out there." If that doesn't give us pause to be exceedingly careful, what will?

Jesus told a crowd, "It is not what enters into the mouth that defiles the man, but what proceeds out of the mouth" (Matthew 15:11). We are responsible for the clime of our hearts and for being mindful of our words. How much more favorable our lives become when we are wise stewards of this gift of language.

Prayer

Word of God, Word of life, of hope, You have provided Your children with the gift of speech, countless words to mix and use like so many hues of paint on a palette. We decide which to spread across the canvas, which will color our destinies and futures. I repent of using my words to hurt or criticize, to ridicule, to gossip and complain. Even when I may be angry, disappointed, sad, frustrated, or afraid, help me use words that are positive and hopeful, extensions of the glorious Truth in my heart.

<u>More scriptures to enjoy and employ</u>

Psalm 17:3; 19:14; 33:6-9; 141:3

Ecclesiastes 10:12

2 Peter 3:5

James 3:1-12

Matthew 12:37; 17:20

Mark 4:39; 7:15

Isaiah 42:9

Proverbs 4:24; 6:2; 10:14; 12:18; 14:3; 18:20-21; 21:23

2 Corinthians 4:13

Hebrews 1:3; 11:3

Joshua 1:8

Revelation 12:11

Chapter 26

How many loaves do you have? Mark 8:5

A call to give

One cold, gray Sunday decades ago, my husband and I decided to whip up a batch of maple bars. We found a recipe, gathered the ingredients, and got busy. After the yeast had done its work, the mound of dough was round and high. Pinching off the recommended amount, we began the process of deep-frying. A sizzling sweetness filled the air. Soon we had a couple dozen bars arrayed on racks to cool. Yet, the bubble of dough looked as big as ever. In fact, it seemed to be growing! We kept at it throughout the afternoon – pinching, frying, cooling, and then placing the bars on waxed paper to await frosting. When every available square inch of kitchen counter was occupied we began arranging them on windowsills, the patio table, wherever we could find room. "When will we ever get to the end of the dough?" we asked ourselves in amazement.

But, at last, late in the day, we dropped the final bit of dough into the oil. At this point it appeared as though there'd been a maple bar invasion. These golden puffy treats were lined up like sentinels on every side.

Looking back, we had our very own multiplication story going on!

Now, let's consider the scene in reference to Jesus' question about the loaves. A crowd of thousands had gathered around our Lord and He desired to feed them. His disciples (relying on the limits of human reasoning) wondered how in the world that could be accomplished. Ignoring their concerns, He inquired, "How many loaves do you have?" We all know what happens next in the story. Our Lord took seven loaves and a few fish, blessed them, distributed them, and the multitudes ate until full.

Today, when we hear the question, "How many loaves do you have?" what we might actually be hearing is, "what do you have to offer?" "What can you contribute to the kingdom of God?" "What will you allow to pass through My hands?" Whatever we have, and are ready to share, offer, and sacrifice, Jesus will bless. And multiply.

Remember the story of the widow's mite? Christ was impressed with this woman's contribution (even though through the lens of human convention it may have seemed quite measly), because for her it was a true sacrifice. We mustn't worry about how our offerings appear (things look different in the spiritual world anyway). It's the willingness to share, the act of love in doing so, and the posture of the heart (God loves a cheerful giver) that reap the harvest.

God just needs <u>something</u> with which to work. At Cana, Jesus turned water into wine. At Capernaum He converted the centurion's words of faith into a healing. Likewise, the seven loaves became food for many thousands. God provides the increase when we make our offering. 1 Corinthians 3:6-7 teaches: "I planted,

Apollos watered, but God was causing the growth. So then neither the one who plants nor the one who waters is anything, but God Who causes the growth."

That is why our tithes are so powerful – they allow God to open up His storehouse of blessing (see Malachi 3:10 and Proverbs 3:9-10).

One couple, long unemployed and living in a motor home, eked out food money by foraging for cans and bottles. One day they attended a church service and desired to share their pittance. With $20 of hard-won food money in their pockets, they prayerfully gave $10. Within two days, the husband had landed a job. Now, some may chalk that up to coincidence, but that $10, in the context of this couple's circumstances, was huge! I imagine it was a seed that propagated many blessings, one of which was a new job.

We don't give to get something – we share because we want to be a blessing. But, we can't out-give God. In some way, not always discernible by the world's metrics, we end up richer and more blessed when we give. Consider, at the conclusion of this meal in Mark 8, there were seven baskets of leftovers! That's more than what they had at the beginning!

And our offerings don't have to be only material. Gifts of talents, time, and self are opportunities for increase as well. Even our attitude can be an offering. Suppose someone is rude to you but, you're in a good mood with a surplus of patience, so responding in love to that person may not be all that imposing. However, if you encounter rudeness or hostility when you are experiencing a shortage of patience or when you've had a trying day, your loving response composes a much more powerful sacrifice.

2 Kings 4:1-7 tells the story of an indebted widow who had but one jug of oil. She was instructed by Elijah to gather up as many containers as she could find. A

supernatural flow of oil continued until all the vessels were filled. I find a striking lesson in the fact that the oil ceased to stream only when the woman had no more room to accept it.

God is a giver, a provider, a meeter of needs. And He is without limit. We are the ones who vary in our capacity to receive.

Truly, there is a connection between hands extended to give and hands open to receive. It is all part of a divine circle of blessing that loops through heaven and earth in an endless spiral.

This principle is beautifully laid out in 2 Corinthians 9:7-14. The first three verses paint a description of a giver. Verse 10 heralds the multiplicative power of God. Then verses 11-14 outline the benefits to God, the giver, and others. This cycle, in simplest terms, is:

1. We give.

2. Our offering is touched by the Lord, increasing as needed.

3. Others are blessed, and so are we.

Maple bars, anyone?

Prayer

Giving God, we are made in Your image, so we are "little givers," at our happiest and most fulfilled when allowing our own gifts to touch others. And what we give with the right attitude is not gone at all, but enhanced, expanded, and energized as it passes through Your hands into areas of need. I count it such a privilege to sow into Your kingdom, into the lives of my brothers and sisters. Show me how to have the mindset of a giver – to see new ways to bless others and honor You.

More scriptures to enjoy and employ

2 Corinthians 9:6-14

Ecclesiastes 11:1

Psalm 112:9

1 Timothy 6:17-19

Hebrews 13:16

James 1:17

Isaiah 58:6-12

Proverbs 11:24

2 Kings 4:42-44

Chapter 27

Why are you reasoning? Mark 8:17 (NAB)

A call to remember, rather than reason

Our minds are fascinating entities, don't you agree? They can work like computers – collecting and sorting data, rumbling around a while, then dispensing "solutions." I've read that information courses through the neurons in our brains at rates up to 268 miles per hour.

When we hear of someone with a problem, or when we have a situation ourselves, we tend towards "what can I <u>do</u>?" Our first inclination may be: "Let's see. This might work," "That might help," or "Maybe I can try such and such." We want to be problem-solvers and fixers, but, too often, we rely on our experience, intuition, and reasoning. Really, God must shake His head at some of our "brilliant" ideas!

Our topic question is a reminder that faith is not predicated on logic. Here, Jesus' disciples had been trying to analyze what he might have meant when He had advised them to watch out for the yeast of the Pharisees. When Jesus asked, "Why are you reasoning?" it is actually the first in a series of eight questions that He fired at His disciples, one after the other (Mark 8:17-21 AMP):

- "Why are you reasoning?"

- "Do you not yet discern or understand?"

- "Are your hearts in hardness?"

- "Having eyes, do you not see, and having ears, do you not hear?"

- "And do you not remember?"

- "When I broke the five loaves for the 5,000, how many baskets full of broken pieces did you take up?"

- "And when I broke the seven loaves for the 4,000, how many baskets full of broken pieces did you take up?"

- "Do you not yet understand?"

Eight links in a chain, these are, conjoined to form a theme: we can't achieve faith propelled by our own understanding and efforts, but by <u>spiritual discernment and remembering</u>. In particular, the fifth question in this series is quite significant. We recall that immediately prior to the events of this moment Jesus had multiplied a humble amount of food into enough to feed thousands. My goodness, these disciples had been witness to a mighty miracle of provision, yet, here they were stressing over a "problem" of having only one loaf in their boat for themselves.

"Do you not remember?" Jesus asked them.

This tendency to forget, minimize, or dismiss what God has said or done for us in the past (spiritual amnesia), and stubbornly put our faith in our own logical reasoning is as old as mankind. Adam and Eve supposed they knew best when they ate of the tree God had declared off limits (Genesis 3:6). Abraham's wife Sarai reasoned (even after God's promise of descendants) that she should allow Hagar, her servant, to bear a child for her husband since she herself seemed unable to conceive. A complicated, ugly mess ensued (see Genesis 16). In Numbers 11, God promised Moses meat enough to feed his great clan of people as they journeyed through the wilderness. Now, keep in mind, this pledge from God came after many acts of deliverance and protection including the parting of the Red Sea, fresh manna every morning, a guiding cloud during the day, and a column of fire by night. Yet, here is what Moses said: "The people around me include 600,000 soldiers ... can enough sheep and cattle be slaughtered for them? If all the fish of the sea were caught for them, would they have enough?" (21-22 NAB)

God responded, "Is this beyond the Lord's reach?"

When we do not remember, we reason.

In Deuteronomy 4:9 (TLB) it is written, "Be very careful never to forget what you have seen God doing for you. May His miracles have a deep and permanent effect upon your lives! Tell your children and your grandchildren about the glorious miracles He did."

This is not to suggest we sit around and do nothing, hesitant to make any kind of decision. God gave us minds to use, and logic certainly has its place. But we are not to be led by reason or emotions-of-the-moment. When we continually figure, plot, plan, and rationalize, our mindset becomes a contorted version of self-reliance (pride) and it is contrary to trusting God. There is a world of difference between a frantic "what can I do?" and a faith-filled "let's witness to what God will do." We are to pray as a first response not a last resort, and then we can proceed as God leads.

Now, remembering God's promises and the lingering, sweet reminiscences of all He has done for us takes conscious effort. But, by doing so, we will find it easier to let God be God. After all, He's much better at it than we could ever hope to be. The prophet Isaiah averred, "'For My thoughts are not your thoughts, nor are your ways My ways,' declares the Lord. 'For as the heavens are higher than the earth, so are My ways higher than your ways and My thoughts than your thoughts'" (55:8-9).

Ultimately, let's know we cannot reason our way to faith. "Reasoning" is earthly, an output of the mind. Faith is heavenly, a product of the Spirit. Trying to arrive at a place of faith by reasoning is like attempting to travel to the moon by train. It won't go there. But, conversely, how exciting it is that faith will take us places reasoning and human logic never could.

Prayer

Faithful Lord, I could come up with a list of questions of my own: Why? When? How will that work? How can I make that happen? What if? Should I? But these questions brim with human reasoning and will just keep me spinning in circles like a dog chasing its tail. Forgive me for the pride that sometimes creeps into my mind – that I know best and that, if I think long and hard enough, I can eventually figure out answers to all of life's dilemmas. The human brain is a wonderful creation but it hasn't been designed to process matters of faith. That is left up to our hearts, our spirit-selves, that part of us in communion with You. Help me to let go of reasoning and embrace the joy and peace that come with remembering

Who You are, how much You love me, and what You continually do for me. Let mine be a faith that rejoices, recognizes, and remembers!

More scriptures to enjoy and employ

Psalm 77:11-13; 78:11-12; 105:5; 106:7; 111; 143:5

Proverbs 3:5-6

Jeremiah 10:23

Matthew 6:33-34

James 1:5-6

Numbers 14:11

Deuteronomy 1:32-33; 7:18-19

John 14:26

1 Samuel 12:24

1 Corinthians 2:14

1 Chronicles 16:12

An added thought: I find that keeping a notebook or set of index cards where I can jot down instances of answered prayers, unexpected blessings, heavenly interventions, "winks" from above is beneficial – the entries a few simple words or, at times, more detailed, coming often or just occasionally.   Re-reading them, particularly during low moments or seasons of challenge is like enjoying "spiritual snapshots" of God's faithfulness.

Chapter 28

What do you want Me to do for you?
Matthew 20:32

*A call to entrust to Jesus our
needs, desires, dreams*

Suppose a mom asks her daughter, "What do you want for your birthday?" And the daughter replies, "I'd love a new sweater!" On her birthday the girl opens up a beautifully wrapped package and pulls out a gorgeous red cardigan sweater with shiny silver buttons. "It's nice," she mutters, "but I was hoping for a white turtleneck."

Of course, this mom had nothing other than a general idea of what her daughter wanted, based on the information given. And even though our heavenly Father knows what we need before we even ask Him (see Matthew 6:8), I believe when we seek after Him with specific requests, needs, desires, and dreams, it allows Him to demonstrate His love in personal and intimate ways.

I was chatting with a friend on the phone one day. A nurse, she'd had an exhaustive, emotionally draining shift and was not looking forward to going back to the hospital the next day. After we hung up I prayed for her.

Now, I could have just said, "God, bless my friend at work tomorrow," and figured I'd done my duty as a Christian friend, but I was led to go deeper. The word that came to me as I interceded on her behalf was "sweet," so I asked the Lord for something "sweet" in her day, a word or event that would uplift her. The next day we spoke again. "The sweetest thing happened at work," she began, and then proceeded to tell me about an incident with a patient.

That's God. He is an involved Father. So tuned in. So faithful. "What do you want Me to do for you?" Jesus asks. Here, in Matthew's Gospel, He is addressing two blind men who, despite having been admonished to keep quiet, shouted to Jesus. This is how they replied to His question: "Lord, we want our eyes to be opened!" And so it happened – another powerful example of "ask and you shall receive" and how the Lord works with trusting hearts.

Obviously, God is not some celestial Santa Claus with a check-off list of our every whim. He knows what is best for us physically, emotionally, spiritually, and on every level, and He is well aware that our inclinations may change as we grow in spiritual maturity. As parents, particularly when our children are young and immature, we certainly do not indulge their every impulse. It would not be in the best interest of a five-year old, for instance, to give him a motor bike, or allow him to stay up late on a school night to watch a scary movie.

But, we need to remember that God concerns Himself with our needs and desires, however noble (or not) they may be. If it's important to us, it's important to Him. And Jesus is as big in our lives as we allow Him to be. So, let's not put limits on Him. Nothing is too huge for Him to handle nor too small for Him to care about. He wants us to come to Him with the granular details of our lives and, as He responds so specifically and so personally, our awareness of His goodness is rocketed to new heights. In Paul's letter to the Philippians, he serves up these warm words: "… in every circumstance and in everything, by prayer and petition (<u>definite</u> requests) with thanksgiving, continue to make your wants known to God" (4:6 AMP). As it is likely that this disciple penned this letter from prison, his description of our Father's enthusiastic interest in each of His children becomes especially trenchant.

My grandmother was a hoot. As a child, I'd look forward to the occasional overnight stay at her house. As she'd scoop food onto my plate she would say, "Tell me 'when.'" Invariably, after I'd say "when," she'd just keep going! An extra pancake, an additional spoonful of rice, one more ladle of her luscious minestrone. To her, "when" meant, "OK, we're getting close."

Gram was a giver. Even more certainly, God is a giver. Scripture tells us He can do "abundantly beyond all that we ask or think" (Ephesians 3:20). He is a Father Who loves blessing His children in mighty and masterful fashion.

Answers to prayer might be quite direct or come about in different, unexpected ways. They may be immediate or follow a period of waiting (growth, germination). The operative principle is that we commend the essentia of our deepest selves to our loving Parent, knowing He can work in us and in our circumstances to ultimately bring about the best possible outcome.

There are instances throughout Scripture where those in positions of power seek to bless or answer the requests of another. In the book of Esther, the king asked this Jewish heroine, "What is your request? Even to half of the kingdom it shall be given to you" (5:3). She appealed for favor, that she and her people would be spared (7:3). In Joshua 15:18, Caleb asked his daughter, "What do you want?" She asked for springs of water, which he granted.

I'd like to draw particular attention to 1 Kings 3:5 (NAB) where Solomon was addressed by God, "Ask something of Me and I will give it to you." Solomon could have requested anything – it was an open invitation – but this king responded that his desire was an understanding heart and the ability to know right from wrong (verses 7-9). So pleased was the Lord that Solomon's intention was to be a good and effective leader for the people entrusted to him, that He not only granted him this prayer, but also riches and honor.

Shall we contrast this to the folly in Eden? The selfish yearning to eat of the forbidden fruit, the tree of the knowledge of good and bad, right and wrong, led Adam and Eve to disaster. Clearly, our motives and level of relationship with God are critical components in what we petition, why we petition, and how God responds.

"What do you want Me to do for you?"

Before we answer this question let us make sure we hold purity of intention and a close fellowship with our Father – in short, a right heart. Not only does this greatly please God, but it is also the surest way to be led along a path of abundance and delight.

I find great joy in 2 Chronicles 16:9 (NAB): "The eyes of the Lord roam over the whole earth to encourage those who are devoted to Him wholeheartedly." One day my family and I were standing in a long line awaiting entrance to our local fair. We happened to have extra tickets and wanted to give them away to someone in the crowd. Our eyes scanned the swarm of people until finally a dad carrying a young child on his shoulders caught our attention. He was very grateful to receive the tickets. Admittedly, we'd been looking at outward appearances; when God's eyes "roam over the whole earth," He is looking at hearts! Simply by living right and carrying love in our hearts we catch the Father's eye. And He has all kinds of "extra tickets," so to speak, to dole out to His children. There is no shortage of blessings where He comes from! Psalm 37:4 (AMP) says, "Delight yourself also in the Lord, and He will give you the desires and secret petitions of your heart." God is privy to secret petitions we might harbor, those not expressed, those we ourselves may not even fully perceive or appreciate. So, He knows better than we do what will gratify our hearts, today and in the future.

Really, how much more awesome could it get than to have the Savior of the world, the Creator of the universe, asking what He can do for us? What need do we have? What desires occupy the hallways of our hearts? He cares. And He's waiting for us to come to Him. Like a child crawling up on a parent's lap, in security, in trust, in anticipation, we are invited to sincerely and humbly share our innermost needs and longings with our Lord amid the blissful understanding that they are important to Him because WE are important to Him!

Prayer

Generous Lord, it is beyond the reaches of my mind how much You love us and absolutely delight in meeting our needs and fulfilling our dreams. That we are so treasured is a constant source of joy. Guide me, like Solomon, to have right and noble desires, to regularly examine my conscience, motives, and goals, to trust You with my heart. It becomes a beautiful, bountiful circle – all of this. When You answer me and work in my life, I begin to see the panorama of Your goodness – and trust You even more with deeper and deeper levels of myself. And You, in turn, are given a door open ever wider through which You can demonstrate Your benevolence.

<u>More scriptures to enjoy and employ</u>

James 4:2

Psalm 81:10-11; 145:19

Philippians 4:19

Deuteronomy 28:1-14

Proverbs 10:24

3 John 1:2

1 John 5:15

Chapter 29

Why are you persecuting Me? Acts 9:4

A call to repentance

Our question here is the only one of the 40 contained in this work that Jesus asks after His ascension into heaven. Saul, a known and feared persecutor of Christians, was on his way to Damascus for the purpose of gathering support in his campaign of destruction. It seems the drive of this egregious intent had taken control of his life.

Suddenly, a brilliant light shone down upon him and the words of our Lord echoed from above: "Saul, Saul, why are you persecuting Me?"

Saul, himself, then asked, "Who are You?"

Even though Saul's eyes were blinded (perhaps because he was mired in such feral darkness at that point that the intensity of the light was overwhelming), he followed Jesus' instructions to enter Damascus. For three days he remained sightless and he neither ate nor drank. The Bible doesn't detail exactly what happened during this time, but given the powerful ways in which

God used him afterward, we can surmise He was knitting Saul's heart to His own. This man's conversion was taking place. (And, quite fittingly, the house where he stayed was on Straight Street!) Finally, on the third day, God sent someone to lay hands on Saul that his vision would return. Verse 20 (AMP) says Saul, also known as Paul (see 13:9), immediately began proclaiming Jesus. He traveled far and wide to preach the message of salvation and eventually became the author of 13 (some sources allege that number to be 14) New Testament books. Truly, Paul knew the impulsion of God's goodness and lived the miracle of a transformed life.

Here we are presented with an opportunity to examine more closely the words *repentance* and *conversion.* We hear of repentance most often in the context of our sins. Its definition is: "deep sorrow; regret for any past action." But, holy repentance doesn't stop there. From a biblical point of view, the Hebrew and Greek words for repentance imply a turn, a change in one's orientation.

Now, let's look at the definition of conversion: "transformation; a change in character, form, or function; spiritual change from sinfulness to righteousness."

So, for the purposes of this writing, we shall recognize that each of these terms necessarily involves change from within.

When we visit a foreign country we can't expect to purchase a meal, a T-shirt, even a postcard with the cash from our native land. In its present form it is utterly useless. We must CONVERT our currency before it can be of any service. Conversions of heart can be sudden or gradual; they can happen in big ways and small, so we are compelled to ask ourselves how it is we might require change so God can fully use us. Some may think, "I already believe in Jesus – I don't need conversion." While our need for conversion may not be as dramatic as in Paul's case, it is safe to say we all have areas and issues that would benefit from change and growth – a turning, of sorts.

A beautiful old painting entitled "The Light of the World" depicts Jesus standing on the outside of a door, as if waiting. There is no knob for Him to use. His right hand knocks; His left holds a bright lantern. Shabby, dry weeds cluster at the base of the door, indicating a lack of activity, but still He waits. As at our hearts, He will knock but we are the ones to TURN the inside knob and allow Him to enter. Revelation 3:20 (NAB) says, "Here I stand, knocking at the door. If anyone hears Me calling and opens the door, I will enter His house ...."

True repentance means we turn FROM something and TO Him, from what is hindering and harmful to new ways of thinking, acting, and approaching life. Conversion invites us to be open to novel ways in which God can lead us. We might be tempted to assume we are unworthy or not "good enough" to serve God. How wrong! With that attitude, who then could ever be qualified? God does not have to wait until we're perfect before He will avail Himself of us. (I'm sure Paul made mistakes even after the momentous events at Damascus.) He must wait, though, until our hearts are right toward Him, until we make that inner turn and open the door.

If Paul, sinful as he was, could be made ready for a great life of ministry which would reverberate through all succeeding generations, so can we be prepared for the futures God has at the ready for us.

A couple of comments Paul made at later times acknowledged an ongoing thankfulness and need for God. Speaking to King Agrippa, Paul referenced the incident at Damascus in Acts 26:19 (NAB): "I could not disobey that heavenly vision." Then, in verse 22, he declares: "I have had God's help to this very day." Paul gave all credit to God when, in his first letter to the Corinthians, he stated, "By the grace of God I am what I am, and His grace toward me was not for nothing. I worked harder than all of them, though it was not really I, but the grace of God which was with me" (15:10 AMP). It is apparent that his new attitude was life-altering – that despite the horrific nature of his former ways, this future saint was a humbled and changed man.

Ask a physicist what the coldest allowable temperature is and she'll tell you, "negative 273 degrees Celsius, absolute zero." It is not possible for matter, as we know it, to become any colder. If we think about it, what we call "cold" is merely the lack of heat just as darkness is the absence of light. A spiritual parallel might offer that evil exists only to the extent that goodness is missing. What happens when God is removed from families, schools, governments, the individual human heart? Time and again we've witnessed the hard lessons of a diminished regard for moral principles – the naïve relativism that so readily seduces.

Paul had been in just such a state of deception as a first-century terrorist out to further his cause of "justice." A cold, dark, evil heart beat within him. Most surely, the sole way to combat cold is to introduce heat, and darkness can only be dispelled by bringing in light. Correspondingly, Romans 12:21 urges us to conquer evil with good.

Simply stated, Paul was overcome by the goodness of God and his metamorphosis yields yet another instruction for us today: Once we repent of past sin, of wrong attitudes, we are to let them go. Sometimes the devil would want to keep reminding us of them over and over (see Revelation 12:10). But, it is implausible that Paul could have accomplished the challenge before him had he been stuck in a circular, continual pattern of remorse – rehashing past mistakes and sins, fueling the fires of regret. Yes, it is helpful to remember and be grateful for God's mercy in forgiving us and leading us to change. We dwell on His goodness; we magnify His willingness to fill us up where we are weak (see 2 Corinthians 12:9), not on our frailties, not on old errors and missteps. Once we've repented and accepted God's forgiveness and mercy, we are not to entertain a cacophony of tormenting, condemning thoughts nor hold onto burdens of sorrow and regret. "If the Son makes you free, you will be free indeed" (John 8:36).

Another hopeful lesson gathered from this study is that we are not to give up on anyone! If you have been praying for someone's conversion and salvation, continue praying even if the situation looks impossible. No one is too far gone. A turnaround can happen in the twinkling of an eye. Keep in mind what happened to Paul within the span of 72 hours! Jesus is at the door!

Prayer

God of new beginnings, help me to dig deep – deep enough to be remorseful over sin, deep enough to make real changes, deep enough to accept Your forgiveness and leave behind that which has stagnated, remembering it's not the past that matters (true conversion means all that has been buried under the blood), it's today's heart. Thank You for waiting at the heart's door of each individual. You are welcome and needed in mine. Please come in and stay!

More scriptures to enjoy and employ

2 Corinthians 3:16; 7:8-10

Joel 2:12-13

Acts 2:38; 3:19; 26:18

Ezekiel 14:6; 18:30-31

Matthew 18:3

Luke 3:8

Romans 2:29

1 Timothy 1:13

Chapter 30

Were not all made whole? Was there no one to return and give thanks except the foreigner? Luke 17:17-18 (NAB)

A call to gratitude and praise

A lovely older woman who owned a tree farm decided to donate some trees one Christmas season. Charities, families in need, and our local hospital, were all recipients of her generosity. When my husband picked up a tree to deliver to the hospital, the woman graciously invited him back to select one for his family. We were so grateful to her that, later, the children and I baked a batch of chewy molasses cookies and wrote a note of thanks. When my husband dropped them off she was touched and shared with him that she had donated 142 trees that year and received only eight cards of appreciation. Most certainly, she hadn't provided these trees to others so she could be thanked and recognized, but it seemed such a striking and sad example of ingratitude.

In this gospel account, Jesus was met by ten lepers who called to Him for mercy. He instructed them to show themselves to the priests, and the entire lot of them was cured along the way. Yet, only one came back to thank the Lord. And what a scene that must have been – this Samaritan man fell prostrate at Jesus' feet, all the while giving glory to God. Here is a man who was deeply grateful. Jesus asks, "Were not all ten made whole? Where are the other nine? Was there no one to return and give thanks to God except this foreigner?"

Assuredly, we are here being asked to consider how often we've sought God's help − only to neglect to thank Him when He answered our prayers. How wise it is to be thankful continually – while we pray, during the wait, and after receiving our answer. 1 Thessalonians 5:14-18 (AMP) lists five "always" directives:

Always keep your temper.

Always aim to show kindness.

Be happy and rejoice always.

Be unceasing in prayer.

Thank God in everything.

Take notice – these do not say to be happy and kind and temperate only when our circumstances are placid, but always. Neither do they command us to thank God for everything but rather we are to thank Him in everything. In the middle of traffic, we can thank Him for our car; surrounded on every side by piles of laundry, for running water and electricity; when we encounter rudeness, we are especially grateful for the wonderful people in our lives; in the midst of trying times, for the beacons of hope and strength. (Sometimes when I'm tempted to be annoyed by my husband's snoring, I remember to thank God for this devoted man, and for my ability to hear!) We can always find something for which to thank Him!

Our Father does not need our thanks for Himself. But He knows we need them. An attitude of gratitude stirs up joy and a fresh new way of looking at things. It keeps us humble because we know our Source and with every word of praise and thanksgiving we offer, we are reminding ourselves of His goodness. Participants in a study in which they were asked to sit down each night and think of three positive things that had happened during the day, reported feeling happier and even sleeping better. Clearly, the benefits of gratitude fathom the physiological, psychological, and social strata of our beings.

Praise and gratitude also impart supernatural advantages. Let's imagine, for a moment, a bride on her wedding day. Her hair, make-up, and nails are impeccable. Her gown flows and her jewelry sparkles. She glows with happiness.

We, the church, are Christ's bride. So, we ask ourselves, how can we look beautiful for Him? One way is by praise! Psalms 33:1 and 147:1 (AMP) say, "Praise is becoming." To a great degree, we do not determine our earthly looks, but isn't it nice to know we can affect how we appear in the supernatural? And, perhaps we are never more beautiful to God than when we are wholeheartedly praising Him.

Praise also can be offered as a spiritual sacrifice. There are many scriptural references which equate praise with sacrifice including Hebrews 13:15. All the ways to thank, pay homage, and show respect to the Lord (some people like to sing, dance, and shout – others might prefer quiet reflection in reading psalms and whispering words of worship), are precious and acceptable as long as the heart is sincere. Further, the Bible tells us God inhabits the praise of His people (explore Psalm 22:3). When we praise, His glory comes on the scene. We remember Jehosophat's situation in 2 Chronicles 20:20-23 when he and his people set themselves to sing and praise on the way to battle. Not only were their enemies utterly destroyed but it took a full three days to carry away the spoils.

Some of the words for "glory" in the Hebrew language translate: "beauty," "majesty," "purity," "preciousness" – in essence, so much that is good about God (see 2 Chronicles 5:13-14 and Isaiah 6:3). What power reigns in the fullness of His presence – what power there is in praise!

Let's study, briefly, another spectacular instance of God's manifested might – the resurrection of Jesus Christ. Romans 6:4 says He was raised by the glory of God. Now, if praise is a catalyst for glory, let's look a little deeper into the Scriptures to see from where praise may have come at that point. Of course there were angels in heaven, but check this out: In Matthew's Gospel account of Jesus' death, we note that many saints were raised up from the tomb at that moment (27:53). And, although the Bible doesn't specifically say so, I like to think that their choir of praise helped usher in the most vigorous display ever of God's glory in the resurrection.

As we conclude, let's briefly revisit our gospel story. In verse 19 Jesus expresses the importance of what this man at His feet has just done: "Stand up and go your way; your faith has been your salvation." We can see there is gratitude on the way to salvation! Praise uplifts and beautifies; it breaks bondages and brings joy; it is a welcome sacrifice to the Lord; it releases glory on site and illumes the path to health and salvation! Let's make thanking, praising, and worshipping our Lord integral chords in the tempo of our lives.

Prayer

Praiseworthy God, thank You for blessings, provision, and answered prayer. I'm ever grateful for Who You are. Teach me to praise and worship You continually and in sincerity, knowing this invites You and all of Your power and goodness into my life.

Additional scriptures to enjoy and employ

Psalm 9:1-3; 18:1-3; 145

Colossians 1:11-12

Philippians 4:4

Romans 4:20

Chapter 31

Did I not say to you that if you believe, you will see the glory of God? John 11:40

A call to open up heavenly places with our faith

I may believe it is always cold in December because that's the way I've known it to be. But, give me a warm sunny December day and suddenly my "belief" is no longer valid. Head-believing is predicated on sensory perceptions, circumstances, and experiences. Heart-believing, on the other hand, is anchored and unmoving for it is founded on something that cannot change – God's word of truth. His love, promises, provisions, and precepts are rock-solid, even amidst the flux of life on Planet Earth. And just how can we tell which one prevails in our thoughts? Here is how: by noticing what is the first thing that rises up inside when facing a crisis or challenge.

Our opening question immediately precedes the account of Jesus raising Lazarus from the dead. Martha, Lazarus' sister, was concerned about the stench from the

151

decaying body after Jesus commanded that the stone covering the tomb be removed. After all, her brother had been dead four days. But that did not concern our Lord and He, in effect, told her that it should not concern her either. What she feared was of the corporeal world – Jesus speaks of the supernatural (which always transcends the natural) – the glory of God. But, take note: He said, "IF you believe." Again, we see that it is faith that taps into the supernatural realm, faith that brings powerful results – outcomes that might not always "make sense to our senses."

Jesus went on to raise Lazarus, something unheard of within the physical domain. How exciting! That Jesus' faith accomplished the most impossible of the impossible means there are no limits to what faith can do.

Notice how the Lord had taken His time getting to the tomb (verses 5-7). I believe this was for the benefit of His followers. After all, the resurrection of Lazarus after FOUR DAYS in the tomb could help generate a faith big enough to cover Jesus' THREE-DAY burial that was to come.

I'm about to offer a concept that might seem a bit convoluted, but hang in there with me. Not only did Jesus teach about faith, *He became our faith*. What do I mean by that? In mathematics we learn the transitive property: if $A = B$ and $B = C$, then $A = C$. (In more concrete terms we can say, "if 10 pennies are equivalent to 2 nickels, and 2 nickels are the same as a dime, then 10 pennies must equal a dime.") Now, check out these scriptures: 1 John 5:4 says *our faith* is the power that has conquered the world. John 16:33 tells us *Jesus* has overcome and conquered the world. So, if Jesus has conquered the world and the world has been conquered by our faith, then we can logically equate Jesus with our faith. Jesus equals our faith. Jesus is our faith!

That is liberating news! It means we can never say, "my faith is not big enough to handle that" or "my faith is too weak." No, HOPE may be feeble (more on this in the following chapter), but our faith is not because Jesus, the Name above every name (Philippians 2:9), and the Author and Source of our faith (Hebrews 12:2), resides in us! If nothing is impossible for Him (Matthew 19:26), nothing is impossible for our faith!

Jesus (our faith) can roll away stones, calm the heaving seas, heal the sick, chase out demons, and rise from the dead. We'll remember that in John 14:12 Jesus tells us the faithful will do the works that He does and ones even greater. In Mark 16:17-18 He says _believers_ will expel demons, handle serpents, lay hands on the sick, and drink poison without harm.

As Jesus did when He commanded Lazarus to come forth, we are to look beyond what we see.

Imagine driving down an old country road when suddenly you hit a giant mud hole and, just like that, your windshield is splattered. Having nothing with you to clean it and knowing your wipers would only smear the mud around and worsen the matter, you make a decision. You choose to continue on and keep your eyes focused on what is beyond the impaired windshield. You "look through" the mud splotches to the road ahead – a wise decision for turning your eyes to the gunk would only blur what lies at a distance.

Isn't it interesting how God created our eyes unable to focus on things near and far at the same time? It's the way, too, of His kingdom. Concentrating on earthly situations and problems, like Martha did, obscures the glory that is but a shift in focus away.

Daily, we ask ourselves, what is my rock – that seemingly unmovable situation? Do I have a stone that needs to be rolled away? And what miracles wait beyond it? Do I dare believe for something big?

Let's find a promise in Scripture that covers whatever need we may have and stand firm on it, no matter how outward circumstances may appear. God is faithful. We tap into the supernatural with faith. Remember, the spirit-world is more real than the natural. The universe, in all its expanse, was cast and set from a spiritual source. It will pass away; the world to come is everlasting. We are invited to believe beyond sensory perception and watch the glory of God! The tomb is open!

<u>Prayer</u>

Father of Glory, it is not Your way that we "test the waters" and then decide if we want to believe, nor is it possible to "look beyond" first, then build our faith upon what we see. In Your kingdom, believing is seeing! Just as our eyes are the means by which we perceive light, color, dimension, and shape, our ears sound, our noses scents, etc., so faith is the channel through which You are experienced. And although humankind uses microscopes, telescopes, corrective lenses, amplifiers, salt, and countless other products, gadgets, and inventions to enhance perception, we still possess a very limited range through which we can process information. There is so much more outside the scope of our five natural senses. But faith has no limit to what it can see, believe for, and accomplish. I dare to believe beyond what my earthly senses might relay. **TRUTH** *trumps facts every time.*

<u>More scriptures to enjoy and employ</u>

John 3:12

Colossians 1:27

1 Corinthians 1:18; 2:14

2 Corinthians 4:6,18

Chapter 32

Do you now believe? John 16:31

A call to Christian hope

When purchasing a digital camera or phone, one may take into account the number of megapixels it offers. As we are aware this terminology refers to a certain type of technology that helps enhance the clarity or crispness of the image. With enough megapixels, even when it is enlarged, the photo or picture won't be grainy or dull, but will stay sharp and vivid.

True Christian hope is like that.

Hope is alive when we are so convinced of God's love and faithfulness that we have a clear "inner knowing." Even when what we are believing for is significant in size, the consciousness of the Lord's goodness is crisp and well defined.

Too often in today's society the word hope is confused with "wish." "I hope I get that job promotion," or "I hope it doesn't rain Saturday." Hope is not wishful thinking. It is WORDful thinking.

Jesus' question to His disciples, "Do you now believe?" came right after they had professed their conviction in Who He is saying, "You know all things" and, "You came from God." To Jesus' relief, His disciples, at last, understood.

In the very next chapter Jesus prayed to the Father: "Now they realize that all that You gave Me comes from You. I entrusted to them the message You entrusted to Me, and they received it. They have known that in truth I came from You, they have believed it was You Who sent Me" (verses 7-8 NAB). Apparently, Jesus needed the disciples to clearly recognize His Source, His purpose, before He would allow Himself to be crucified. He was relying on them to carry on the message. Our omniscient Lord foresaw their scattering and desertion so He asked them our topic question which, in one translation, is worded, "Do you FINALLY believe?" (NLT) They had the knowledge, even the faith, but was their hope such that it could withstand the terrors ahead? Did they truly have an inner picture of God's sovereign goodness?

Directed at us, this question might suggest our need to consider the lucidity of our own image of the Lord. Do we believe Jesus only when we think we understand – or do we believe no matter what? Does our hope become murky when we encounter challenge – or does it remain sharp as ever so faith can work? Hope is the blueprint, the girder for faith – that upon which it is built. We are so convinced of God's favorable intentions toward us that, even when we can't perceive how a situation could ever possibly be resolved, turned around, or resurrected, we can still have hope. We may not know HOW, but we know WHO.

In Genesis 15 God promised Abram many descendants. Now, he and his wife Sarai were quite old and didn't know HOW this could possibly come about – but Abram knew WHO. Two chapters later God deemed name changes to be in order. Abram became Abraham,

"Father of a multitude of nations," and Sarai, Sarah, "Mother of nations." Imagine – every time their names were spoken they heard the promise of God. Romans 4:18-21 (NLT) says, "Even when there was no reason for hope, Abraham kept hoping – believing that he would become the father of many nations. For God had said to him, 'That's how many descendants you will have!' And Abraham's faith did not weaken, even though, at about 100 years of age, he figured his body was as good as dead – and so was Sarah's womb. Abraham never wavered in believing God's promise. In fact, his faith grew stronger, and in this he brought glory to God. He was fully convinced that God is able to do whatever He promises."

I believe Abraham was able to remain so strong in faith because he had hope – hope in a God Who had always been faithful and close. We'll recall that when God presented that promise to Abraham He took him outside and challenged him to look up and count the stars saying, "So shall your descendants be." And even though the first dawning of that promise's fulfillment, the birth of Isaac, didn't occur until a dozen or so years later, we can suppose that if Abraham ever felt he was becoming doubtful, this vista of a brilliant starry night sky might have kindled the fire of his faith – the faith that was needed to secure the promise.

I love the way Jesus, too, used real-life, real-world examples of heavenly principles during His earthly ministry. His stories certainly bring His points into vibrant focus. The prodigal son, the lost sheep, the good Samaritan – the Gospels burst with parables and revelations, analogies and accounts, all of which combine to paint a striking, crystalline picture of our God's love and goodness.

Faith that is saturated with hope is powerful indeed. Conceive the joy, the effectiveness of a faith that roots down in the soil of eternal hope. One of the words for hope Paul uses in the Greek language is defined, "The happy anticipation of good." As Christians, every day we ought to bubble forth with hope, with the happy anticipation of good!

Prayer

Lord of our hope, thank You for rainbows and flowers, smiles and happy songs – outward signs of hope. Even more, thank You for Your unlimited, unfailing, unmatched goodness, the source of our inner hope. Help me to see Jesus in me, clearly and constantly, and to comprehend that genuine Christian hope is a great empowerer to live strong in faith.

More scriptures to enjoy and employ

Jeremiah 17:7-8

Philippians 1:19-20

2 Corinthians 3:12-18

Ephesians 2:12-13

Hebrews 6:19; 11:1

Hosea 12:6-7

Romans 8:24-25

Chapter 33

Why are you troubled and why do doubts arise in your hearts?   Luke 24:38

A call to peace

One morning my 3-year old nephew and I were playing on the back lawn when, unexpectedly, the sprinkler heads popped up and began spraying! I scooped him up and darted to dry ground. In all the commotion, he was frozen, not knowing how to respond. It was only when he saw me laugh that he relaxed and began to laugh as well. Not able to judge the seriousness (or not) of the situation, he had looked to me for a cue on how to react.

Now, let's consider this gospel moment. The resurrected Jesus appeared to His disciples and said, "Peace be to you." How did the disciples respond? Ironically, with fear and panic, thinking He was a ghost! That's when Jesus posed this question, "Why are you troubled?" Then He said, "See My hands and feet, that it is I."

Had the disciples accepted the peace Jesus offered I am quite certain they would have seen Him for Who He is, for peace brings clarity – but they did not accept it, so they were confused and fragmented by fear. General biblical definitions for peace include "freedom from disturbance, outwardly and inwardly, to be still or silent." I love that description – stillness.

A mountain lake can be a natural mirror for its surroundings when the water is still and serene. Not so when the waters are choppy and tumultuous – the reflected images are distorted and changing. Without peace everything is a struggle. Nothing is clear. Similarly for us, when our souls are bathed in peace things are seen as they are. Our judgment is keener. Our ability to hear from God is sharper.

Colossians 3:15 (AMP) implores us to let peace be our umpire. Now, an umpire is trained to make accurate calls – to be clear in judgment. When peace is our umpire, our discerner, we craft decisions that are purposeful and appropriate, not haphazard and random. We view things definitively.

One spring morning I was walking across a supermarket parking lot when a bird brushed across the back of my head. I didn't pay much attention to it until a bit later when I was exiting the store. That same bird was attacking others – people strolling across the lot, shoppers placing bags of groceries in their trunks. This little feathered fellow flitted about them, nervously and aggressively, then dive-bombed their heads! Apparently, it had a nest nearby and perceived anyone in the vicinity as a threat. The bird certainly had no peace, exhausting itself with continual attacks against "predators," waging a frenzied battle no one else was the least bit interested in. Imagine how much more peaceful the bird's day might have been had it simply remained "still."

Sisters and brothers, we *do* have an enemy, one that comes to "steal, kill, and destroy" (see John 10:10). But, Philippians 1:28 (AMP) tells us not to be frightened or intimidated by anything and that our fearlessness is actually a portent to our enemies not only of their destruction, but also of our deliverance. Wow! It's no wonder literally hundreds of "Do not be afraids" and "Fear nots" dot sacred Scripture like so many daisies in a meadow.

Let's reference again the episode of Jesus rebuking the storm. We'll remember He'd been sound asleep in the boat when the wind and waves grew intense. The peace inside of Him was channeled through His faith-filled words into the outside conditions and the storm abated.

Jesus never lost His peace, despite horrific circumstances – the stormy sea, the devil's temptation, the failures of those around Him, the crucifixion. He remained steady in the midst of tumult and pandemonium. He held His peace, that inner calm, that stillness. John 14:27 (TLB) explains that Jesus gave us peace as a *gift* – it is indeed something we accept and to which we cleave: "I am leaving you with a gift – peace of mind and heart! And the peace I give isn't fragile like the peace the world gives. So don't be troubled or afraid." Yet, too often we allow concerns about jobs, finances, family, relationships, global crises, and other matters to chisel away at this gift of peace and to impede our spiritual progress.

The story of Martha and Mary in Luke 10 beautifully contrasts the two extremes of unrest and peace. Jesus told Martha, "You are worried and bothered." Martha, we'll remember, was frantic with taking care of details – the particulars of hospitality, dinner, and household chores. Mary, on the other hand, seated herself at Jesus' feet and listened to Him. Martha seemed more interested in trivia, Mary in truth.

Verse 10 of Psalm 46 is one of the best directives for peaceful, undisturbed living in all of Scripture: "Cease striving and know that I am God."   Another translation presents a rich quarry of meditations:

"Be still and know that I am God." (NLT)

Be still and know that I AM.
Be still and know.
Be still.
Be.

Lest we think such peace is unattainable in today's world, reading Galatians 5:22 we are reminded peace is one of the fruits of the spirit. That means, for believers, not only is peace a gift, but it is already inside us. Jesus has provided the seed-germ of peace and, like Him, we are not to be distracted or tempted away from what is already there.

Witness, with me, the nucleus of kingdom peace resonating through our Lord's words from John 16:33 (AMP): "In the world you have tribulation and trials and distress and frustration." He doesn't sugarcoat the reality. Yet, in that very same verse He had just said: "In Me you may have perfect peace."   Jesus continues, "I have overcome the world. I have deprived it of power to harm you and have conquered it for you." In the world, there's trouble.   In Him, there is peace.   Do we get how exceedingly simple it all is?

In conclusion, we look again at Jesus' question: "Why are you troubled?" He would not ask that if the way of peace had not been securely provided and illuminated for us. Think of a tiny baby snuggly strapped to his dad's chest in a carrier. See the dad walking along, watching out for traffic, vicious dogs, etc., and all the while the child is perfectly content and trusting, insulated from the cold and other "dangers" he doesn't even realize are so near. We have the powers of heaven – the promises of

God – working on our behalf. He has conferred on us His perfect peace. Nothing should disturb us. I like how the Living Bible in Psalm 112:7 describes the attitude of the righteous man: "He does not fear bad news, nor live in dread of what may happen. For he is settled in his mind that Jehovah will take care of him." Settled. Peaceful.

Let's journey all the way back to the opening verses of the Bible. There is a dark and windy abyss, a formless wasteland, aptly characterizing the condition of many disturbed souls today. From this murky mess God composed our world. Appropriately enough, in the first event recorded in our Holy Book, order and beauty are brought forth from chaos. Our God is the God of peace.

Prayer

Prince of peace, I praise You for Your peace and Your protection. I thank You for rescuing me when I've called upon You and also when I've been in trouble and not even known about it. You are a doting Father Who will always take care of His children. Help me to embrace the peace You have provided. When I do my life will better reflect my Savior. It's a choice. I can live in peace or I can live in panic. I think it is much easier for You to take care of me when I am at peace. And it's easier for me to make clear decisions and to see the path of Your will, without the clutter and confusion of fear, doubt, and worry.

More scriptures to enjoy and employ

Isaiah 9:6; 26:3,12

Philippians 4:6-7

Romans 5:1

Psalm 71:15; 107:29

Numbers 6:24-26

Chapter 34

Why are you weeping?   John 20:15

A call to know He is with us

What would you think about someone who, every time you shed a tear for whatever reason, comes and gently slides it off your cheek and into a bottle? What if your tears are so precious to him that he won't let even one get by? Can we fathom such tenderness? Well, I've just described our heavenly Father. Psalm 56:8 tells us He records and stores our tears ….

"Why are you weeping?" Jesus asked Mary Magdalene as she stood at His empty tomb. Mourning the Lord, she wanted to know where His body had been taken. But, even as He asked her this question, she neither saw nor recognized Him.

Why do we weep? What brings us to tears? And would we be weeping if we recognized that Jesus is so near?

Something curious happens when cities become large and "hardened," when trees, grassy fields, and native plant life give way to acres of concrete structures and high-density grids of paved roadways and sidewalks.

These artificial materials absorb and trap heat energy in such a way as to actually alter the natural climate. When conditions are right, cooler air from peripheral rural areas is drawn in, creating an updraft and urging on the formation of rain clouds. We might maintain that when the Holy Spirit – Who is alive in our hearts – is stifled by grief or condemnation (or any other foreign condition we allow access), the soul-environment is disrupted. You see, our "natural climate," so to speak, is joy. Joy is a fruit of the spirit, ours when we accept Christ.

In John 16:33 (AMP) our Lord tells us to "be of good cheer." In the same translation Psalm 94:19 reads, "In the multitude of my anxious thoughts within me, Your comforts cheer and delight my soul." It is clear and certain that, even though we may endure times of trial, we are not created to be a people of sorrow. Yes, we weep with remorse for our sins (Joel 2:12) and with empathy for the pain of others (Romans 12:15). We'll note, too, that Jesus, Himself, wept with a troubled heart when He learned of the death of Lazarus (John 11:35). So, while Ecclesiastes 3:4 mentions "a time for weeping," we go on to read in Revelation 7:17 and 21:4 that God will wipe away every tear. We are promised in Psalm 126 that ultimately our tears are turned into joy. Because of Jesus we are an Easter people! Our forecast is joy with a 100% chance of more joy!

What Jesus asks in Matthew 9:15 (AMP) is of particular interest here: "Can the wedding guests mourn while the bridegroom is still with them? The days will come when the bridegroom is taken away from them, and then they will fast." He is telling us in straightforward terms that as long as He (the bridegroom) is with us there should be no mourning. Now, let's consider that thought under the light of His words in Matthew 28:20 (TLB): "… and be sure of this – that I am with you <u>always</u>, even to the end of the world." In essence we read, "You can cry when I'm gone, but I'll never really be gone."

Mary Magdalene wept because she missed Jesus and thought He was gone. We recall that she used her tears to wash our Lord's feet in the seventh chapter of Luke, verse 38. In John 13 we learn there is a biblical significance to the act of feet washing. It is a sign of humility and service, a rite of cleansing and purification – even so far as to be associated with baptism. I find it especially significant that here, at the tomb, her tears are once again a focus for our Lord.

And we can only imagine Mary Magdalene's utter excitement when she finally recognized Jesus, for off she ran to the disciples to spread the word. How quickly her tears must have disappeared.

The Tower of Babel (described in Genesis 11) was a pride-inspired structure intended to reach heaven. The builders of this crudely engineered skyscraper angered God and He brought upon them confusion in their language. The reason our Father was so displeased then is a cogent point of study here. He does not want us trying vainly to access Him by our own works and toil. WE HAVE A GOD WHO COMES TO US. He came to us in the body of a man. He continues to be present in the Person of the Holy Spirit.

Our every tear is chronicled and accounted for – tears of sorrow, joy, frustration, regret, pain, fear – they are all safe in His keeping. And while the Lord is sympathetic to our tears, it greatly honors Him when we pray with confidence and joy, no matter our circumstances, no matter our feelings, knowing His power to help, to heal, and to uplift is greater than any challenge the world might throw our way. He is the Overcomer. And He is right here.

Prayer

Near and dear Lord, thank You for being right here in our midst, so intimately that not a tear goes unnoticed. When we are feeling most alone and vulnerable Your bottle is open to cradle our tears, Your arms are open to hold and comfort, Your grace is open to forgive, heal, and strengthen. Thank You for the joy of Your presence.

More scriptures to enjoy and employ

Psalm 16:11; 30:11-12; 119:151; 126:5

Matthew 5:4

Isaiah 25:8; 61:3

Ephesians 2:13

Jeremiah 31:16

Deuteronomy 4:7

Chapter 35

Did I not choose the 12 of you Myself?
John 6:70 (NAB)

*A call to know we are chosen (and to
make right choices ourselves)*

A tax collector, a political extremist, an assortment of fishermen, and so on the list goes. When Jesus selected His first disciples, what a diverse (some might even say "oddball") group they were! We see throughout the Gospels that Jesus had to deal with their greed, jealousy, doubt, pride, and strife. Unlikely as they might have seemed to accompany God's Son, they were, in fact, just right. Our Lord looked beyond worldly standards into furthering the kingdom of God. He knew what was needed and He knew what He was doing.

And, likewise, He knew what He was doing when He selected us. He was well aware we wouldn't do everything perfectly, that we would have quirks and weaknesses, but also that our collective personalities, talents, and strengths would lend form to His body here on earth. Each Christian brings a contribution no one else can.

Jeremiah 1:5 tells us: "Before I formed you in the womb I knew you, and before you were born I consecrated you." And so we ask ourselves, for what purpose? What has He chosen me to do? What part of the completion of His kingdom is my calling?

Generally speaking, God has chosen us "to go and bear fruit." In an earlier section we took a look at the fruits of the Spirit listed in the fifth chapter of Galatians. More specifically, there are tasks that each member is uniquely equipped to accomplish. Sometimes this all seems clear; at other times we may wonder. But God often works "behind the scenes" (without our being fully mindful of how He might be using us), so the necessity to remain prayerful and obedient is underscored.

"Who wants to accompany the first graders on their field trip?" a teacher asks her fourth grade class. "I need two volunteers." Immediately arms shoot into the air, waving like a choppy sea. Whom will she choose? Which students will she pluck from this flurry of enthusiasm?

This is an appropriate juncture to consider the importance of our own choices. Let's begin by regarding our model, Jesus. No "PICK ME" signs flashed over the heads of His soon-to-be disciples. No hands were raised in eager willingness. So, how did the Lord know which men were to walk with Him and be His close friends? We can find the answer by looking at Scripture. Just prior to the selection of the first disciples (Matthew 4:18-22), Jesus spent 40 days and 40 nights fasting, remaining in the Father's presence, resisting temptation, declaring the Word of God. Luke 6:12 (NAB) tells us, "Then He went out to pray, spending the night in communion with God."

He prayed.

He kept His peace.

He allowed time; He didn't simply say, "Father, help Me choose," and then go about His business. He communed with Father God, in the bosom of His ambrosial companionship, all night. He listened.

We may not have to pray through the night about what shirt to wear or a menu for dinner, but the more time we spend with God meditating, reading Scripture, and truly listening with the heart, the clearer all of our decisions become. Jesus' example is this: A good choice is a prayerful choice.

God chooses us. We choose how to live. He didn't fashion us as marionettes dangling from a string, helplessly obedient. Yes, He desires our obedience and, in fact, requires it to fulfill the bright futures He has in wait for His children, but He will not force us to comply. Our obedience must originate in our free will. He has written a prescription for a happy, prosperous life – we "fill" that prescription by the choices we make. In Deuteronomy 30:19 He says, "I have set before you life and death, the blessing and the curse. So choose life."

Simply, the choices we made yesterday have helped sculpt the life we have today. Those we make today will shape our tomorrows.

Really, nothing is insignificant. What seems like an inconsequential decision to us actually may be quite life-changing. Repercussions ripple far out into the realm of the unseen future. Thus, it is crucial that we seek guidance and direction in all choices – from friendships to finances, health to hobbies, business to ballots – that we pray "without ceasing" as 1 Thessalonians 5:17 instructs which, in essence, means nothing more or less than staying in tune with the Holy Spirit as Jesus did during His earthly life. And, our Father really does make it so simple:

He shows us our path (Psalm 16:11 AMP: "You will show me the path of life").

He <u>lights</u> our path (Psalm 97:11 AMP: "Light is sown for the righteous and strewn along their pathway").

He <u>levels</u> our path (Isaiah 26:7 NAB: "The way of the just is smooth; the path of the just You make level.").

He <u>holds our feet</u> to the path (Psalm 66:9 TLB: "For He holds our lives in His hands, and He holds our feet to the path.").

How excellent it is to know our lives are not accidents. We are not here by chance, but by divine choice. You and I have been hand-picked to be a part of something much bigger than ourselves, the cadence of God's universe.

<u>Prayer</u>

Prudent, judicious Lord, during Your time on earth You made decisions carefully and prayerfully. I recognize that my choices, great and small, fit into a larger context and so should be considered carefully and prayerfully, as well. Herein lies one of the benefits of having Your word in my heart (John 15:7). It is a constant light of clarity upon situations and circumstances. Even so, I will not be flawless in every judgment. If I head down a path not intended for me I rely on You to gently and mercifully come and get me and lead me to where I need to be. I know You do not expect perfection in all of my decisions but You do expect my heart to be perfect toward You, desiring to live in a way that gladdens You. Father, I am forever grateful to be Your chosen child. That the Creator of all that is good has selected me to be a part of His plans and purposes is thrilling to think about! Thank You for my place here and for Your wisdom and guidance.

More scriptures to enjoy and employ

Deuteronomy 30:15-16

Psalm 25:4-5; 33:15; 105:43

John 15:16,19

1 Corinthians 12:12-13,27

Ephesians 1:4

1 Thessalonians 1:4

Isaiah 43:1

Chapter 36

Where did they all disappear to? Has no one condemned you? John 8:10 (NAB)

A call to forgiveness

As he took the first ever steps on the moon, Neil Armstrong's words formed one of the most recognized sound bites in history: "This is one small step for a man, one giant leap for mankind."

From this moment we can draw an analogy relating to humankind's need for God's forgiveness. While a few men nailed Jesus to the cross in a LITERAL way, all of us put Him there in a SPIRITUAL sense. He took upon Himself the guilt, offenses, and death of each person (see Isaiah 53:6, Hebrews 2:9).

Forgiveness is a mighty force. Looking at our topic question, one can only imagine the burden that was lifted from this woman. Here is an adulteress, caught in an act punishable by death. She is literally set free by the forgiveness Jesus extends to her.

We can have the same power of forgiveness in our lives – both when we receive it and when we offer it. But it all begins with receiving, and bedding this deep into our spirits: that no matter what we've done or how far we've strayed from where we should be, God's forgiveness anticipates us, just as the father of the prodigal son in Luke 15 watched and waited for the day his son would return so he could release his heart's hunger to forgive.

I envision a large storehouse in heaven bursting with the mercy of God. To tap into it we must repent of our sins and failures and ask God to forgive us. Because of what Jesus has done on our behalf (in bearing our sins and weaknesses), it is that simple. We ask with a sincerely repentant heart and it is ours. To recap an earlier point of study, we'll recall repentant means "ready to be transformed." It does not mean thinking it is permissible to keep committing the same sin over and over as long as we say we are sorry afterwards.

Over lunch one afternoon, an acquaintance revealed to me that she was about to do something quite drastic that she believed was wrong and contrary to God's will for her. "I'll confess to Him afterward," she said. Friends, we are not to use God's mercy and forgiveness like a bottle of cleaner to mop up messes we make with full intent. Receiving God's forgiveness requires pure heart-motives and a desire to do what is right in the first place.

And, once we've been cleansed by the forgiveness of God, we mustn't allow ourselves to be shackled by thoughts of guilt and regret. In my state, someone who has received a speeding ticket may opt to take an instructional class that keeps the violation from appearing on his driving record. The class, in essence, wipes clean the slate so there are no negative consequences from the citation such as increased insurance rates. God's word says He remembers our sins no more (Hebrews 8:12). I love Psalm 103, which assures us: "As far as the east is from the west, so far as

He removed our transgressions from us" (verse 12). If God is not fretting about our past mistakes, why should we? Guilt and regret are twin monsters with which no child of God should have to live. We are loosed from such bondage by God's love, washed by the blood of Jesus, made new by divine mercy. The sacrificial Lamb has borne our shame (Hebrews 12:2). If, then, we won't forgive ourselves after God has gone to such great lengths to provide the channel for forgiveness, I daresay, what pride! To think our feelings are more powerful or our standards more lofty than the truth of God's Word is indeed prideful.

Let's go back to Jesus' question and notice the words "DISAPPEAR" and "CONDEMN" in reference to this woman's accusers. When God forgives us, our sins are erased – not just covered up or tucked away. Jesus' choice of words here is very relevant. He might as well be saying to us, "Where did your *sins* disappear to? There are none left to condemn you!" Eons apart are the condemnation spewed by the accuser (satan), which heaps upon us a stifling onus of guilt, and the gentle, persistent conviction of the Holy Spirit, which encourages an ongoing examination of conscience and leads to repentance and grace.

The human character leans toward sin – the path of least resistance. In Romans 7:19 Paul says, "For the good that I want, I do not do, but I practice the very evil that I do not want." And Jesus warns Peter in Matthew 26:41, "The spirit is willing but the flesh is weak." God does not expect perfection but He does count on a heart that is sensitive and seeking towards Him. I heard a joke once that illustrates this point: "A man told God, 'Father, so far today I've done okay. I haven't gossiped, cursed, lost my temper, or treated anyone unfairly, but I'm going to be getting out of bed soon and then I'm really going to need Your help!'"

We need God. We need the strength He provides. And, when we slip, we need to be quick to repent and receive His forgiveness. Lamentations 3:22-23 assures us that God's mercies and compassions are new every morning. I don't know about you, but I drink in a good, healthy dose each day!

A couple of chapters ago we touched on that extraordinary moment when Mary Magdalene washed the feet of Jesus with her tears. Let's consider that our Lord's feet must have been in quite a state for in Luke 7:44 He admonishes Simon that no water had been given Him for His feet. Who knows how many miles Jesus walked that day and over what type of terrain? Who can say how hot it might have been or how uncomfortable his sandals were? Yet, the gentle stream bathing His feet fell from the eyes of a penitent woman. Would you agree that her humility, brokenness, and gratitude became tears that blessed our Lord? I am certain God is touched when we humbly accept His forgiveness.

Moreover, when a sinful choice we've made has directly impacted or hurt someone, we must ask their forgiveness. These moments can be uncomfortable but perhaps less so when approached prayerfully and with humility. Serving up an earnest apology – without excuses or rationalizations – and, when possible and appropriate, making reparations for any loss we may have effected are key considerations in seeking forgiveness from another. We then are able to surrender to God's hands how our offering of contrition is received.

All of that said, it is only when we understand how deep our own need for forgiveness goes, and when we embrace the stain-removing sacrifice of Jesus as our own, that we can sincerely and genuinely forgive others. The Bible makes it clear that extending forgiveness is not just a suggestion, but a command. Matthew 6:14 and 18:35, Mark 11:25, and James 2:13 relay just how important it is to forgive so that we can be forgiven. None of the above scriptures specifies which sins we are to forgive and which we are not. Mark 11:25 tells us, "Forgive, if you have anything against anyone." That pretty much covers every possibility, situation, and contingency. We are to forgive all – even to the point of no longer being offended (Psalm 119:165 AMP) – a tall order, to be sure, but what a wonderful example we have in Christ.

Human nature is such that we want to wait until we "feel" all right about the situation, until we "feel" ready to forgive, until we receive an apology or have had sufficient time to calm down and convince ourselves that forgiveness is merited. Yet, waiting to disentangle the emotional loops and knots (which actually can grow tighter when we talk about, think about, and relive how we were wronged) is not a reliable approach at all. Feelings can be fickle, demanding restitution, contorting our good sense. Whether or not the perpetrator deserves to be forgiven is not for us to decide. God is Judge and Vindicator. A much better posture to assume is that while forgiving them in no way suggests we condone what they've said or done, it is an act of Christian duty, an act of the will, indeed, a move of obedience <u>before</u> we might feel like doing so. And that is actually what the word forgiveness means – to give beforehand. WE FORGIVE BY CHOICE, NOT BY FEELING.

It is helpful to have made that choice even before any offense takes place. For instance, let's say someone has decided to arise a half hour earlier each morning to exercise. When his alarm goes off he may not <u>feel</u> like getting up to work out, but because he has purposed beforehand to do exactly that, it is much easier to follow through. A quality, intentional decision made in advance will administrate our behaviors and attitudes. In fact, if we begin each day with the conviction that we will take no offense, and that we will forgive anyone who hurts us, the battle is half over before it has even begun.

A story in the news several years ago featured an Amish community offering forgiveness to the man who murdered five of their school children. They conveyed such gentleness and piety in the aftermath of such unthinkable cruelty (even setting up a fund to aid the murderer's wife and three children), that the world stood up and took notice.

Thankfully, most of us will never find ourselves in such a horrid situation but in all likelihood we will encounter rude and thoughtless remarks, insensitive attitudes, and opportunity after opportunity to be irritated or offended. And sometimes the little things can be what trip us up (see Solomon 2:15). A hurtful comment or action by a co-worker, friend, family member, or stranger can fester in the soul and generate an undercurrent of hostility. And the irony is that these individuals may be totally unaware of their impropriety and just going about their business while we stew.

One of the clearest and most succinct ways to forgive someone is found in three small words within the Gospel of Mark: "Let it drop," beseeches Jesus (11:25 AMP). The beauty of this statement is its profound simplicity. That is all we have to do – let go. When we are clutching an object in our hands and then release it, we are no longer in control of it. Gravity takes over. When we hold tight to shards of unforgiveness, God can't help us. It is only when we "let it drop" that we are freed and He can take over as our Vindicator, Comforter, and Guide.

Allow me to inject a note of clarification at this point. No part of this discussion is to imply that as Christians we let ourselves be doormats for abuse. Obviously there are situations and dynamics that call for some type of action or intervention. The core thought here is that for offenses, great or small, with or without an apology, or even absent the transgressor's remorse or awareness of the hurt he's caused, we are to forgive because that's what Jesus does.

Unforgiveness can be like a roadblock lodged in our spirits – when it is removed our prayers become more effective, our peace more secure, and there is room for us to receive the forgiveness WE may seek from our heavenly Father. Moreover, according to Matthew 5:44, we are to pray for those who persecute us. When Job interceded before God for the very friends who had vilified him, the Lord blessed him with double the prosperity he had previously known (42:10). Our prayers for others, even those we must deliberately wrest from our headstrong will, do not go unnoticed before God.

In conclusion, we contemplate these exigencies of the responsive Christian life – we are not to rehash or keep a list of hurts, nor are we to speak evil of others and harbor grudges. We ARE called to be quick to repent and keep a tender conscience, extend mercy to others in whatever capacity is called for, and allow God to show Himself as our Vindicator. All of this is possible, we recognize, only because ultimately it is not our own but God's power through us that allows us to forgive and be forgiven.

Prayer

Forgiving Lord, I can never "earn" the forgiveness You freely offer through Your Son, but I can receive it, and allow it to encourage and strengthen me when I am faced with a challenge to forgive. I can remember, with deepest gratitude, that even though my sins and missteps nailed You to the cross, I am forgiven. And, so, I can make the decision to allow the reliable current of Your mercy to flow through me, carrying away all forms of unforgiveness, gnawing resentments, bitterness, or an appetite for revenge. Lead me to pray for those who have hurt me with a genuine desire for their good.

More scriptures to enjoy and employ

Psalm 86:5

2 Corinthians 2:11

Romans 2:4; 12:19

Proverbs 17:9; 20:22; 25:21-22

Isaiah 1:18; 54:17

Matthew 5:44

Revelation 1:5; 12:10

Acts 24:15-16

Luke 23:34

Chapter 37

Have I been so long with you, and you have not come to know Me? John 14:9

A call to intimacy with God

A man, absorbed in a newspaper, came across an article he couldn't wait to share with his wife: "Honey, listen to this! A study revealed that men speak an average of 15,000 words a day while women speak 30,000 – twice as many!" He chuckled from behind the newspaper.

"There is an easy explanation for that statistic," replied his wife, "We have to repeat everything we say!"

The man lifted his eyes over the top of the paper. "What?" he asked.

This joke circulated a while back, illustrating an age-old dilemma – not only in marriages, but in other relationships as well: communication glitches.

It seems Jesus Himself is facing a communication quandary of sorts in this question. Let's look at His words in John 14:7 directed to His disciples: "If you had known Me, you would have known My Father also; from now on you know Him, and have seen Him." Basically,

Jesus was saying, "If you've seen Me, you've seen the Father. If you know Me, you know the Father."

It sounds clear and simple, yet immediately Philip implored Jesus to "show us the Father." Alas, Philip was guilty of what so many of us are from time to time. We listen with half an ear, a mind filled with distractions, a heart not fully engaged. Had Philip really listened to Jesus – and not only to these words but also to what He had been saying and demonstrating all along – how confidently he could have accepted that Jesus and the Father are, indeed, one.

So then the Lord asked, "Have I been so long with you, and you have not come to know Me?" At this point, although I believe they loved Jesus, the disciples' hearts lacked the quality of relational intimacy.

Intimacy can be described as "a deep connectedness; the state of knowing and being known." And so we see in Jesus' question it is not necessarily the amount of time we spend with someone that grows true intimacy, but the way that time is spent, the degree to which we make the effort to know and to allow ourselves to be known. Obviously, increasing tiers of intimacy rightfully should come only with deepening trust. To be intimate in any way with someone who is not trustworthy can be disaster. Conversely, an intimate, personal association, an atmosphere of familiarity and comfort with One Who is completely trustworthy is a gift and a privilege. And who is more honorable, more desiring of our companionship, than the Lord Jesus?

Also in John's gospel, Jesus asked some Jews who believed in Him, "Why do you not understand what I am saying?" (8:43) Then He answered the question Himself: "It is because you cannot bear to hear My word" (NAB). Other translations put it like this: "Your ears are shut to My teaching," or "It is because you are prevented from doing so." He went on to speak of the devil's influence over these people, referring to him as "the father of lies." In verse 47, our Lord continued: "Whoever is of God hears every word God speaks. The reason you do not hear is that you are not of God" (NAB). Here, then, is a direct answer from the mouth of our Lord: listening begets understanding and understanding, closeness.

It is interesting that marriage counselors may work to improve intimacy between a husband and wife by targeting communication skills. One of the strategies a therapist might try is to have each spouse, in turn, LOOK at the person who is speaking, LISTEN with focus to what he/she is saying, and REPEAT BACK the meaning of his/her words.

To improve the texture of our intimacy with the Lord, we can employ that same technique. We can LOOK, keeping the eyes of our heart on Him. We can LISTEN, paying careful attention to His words. We can REPEAT BACK by speaking and acting on those words in our lives.

We know from experience that if we try to listen to someone while reading, texting, watching TV, or engaging in some other activity, or with preconceived notions about what he/she is saying, or while absorbed in what we will say next, our listening is affected. Meanings are lost or distorted. Communication problems can escalate in marriages, family or business relationships, and friendships.

Similarly, our faith-lives require time, attention, and effort. How do we score? Answering this question brings us back to how we would respond to our opening query: "Have I been so long with you, and you have not come to know Me?" and it might mean taking a good, hard look at ourselves now and then:

- When we read the Bible, are we intent and focused or do our minds wander?

- When we pray, are we seeking God's face and an intimate dialogue or are we distracted by what we need to do? Might we even fall asleep?

- When we go to church, are we attentive and fully participating or do we spend our time scanning the congregation, or maybe compiling a mental shopping list for a stop at the store on the way home?

- When we interact with others, do we endeavor to see the Lord in them or are we mostly concerned with taking care of business and moving on?

We must put in the effort (God always does His part) to build an intimate fellowship with Him. Let's LOOK at Him, LISTEN to Him, and REPEAT BACK through our own lives the wonderful truths of what we learn, recognizing we belong to each other, He to us and we to Him. And, through times and years, as we know Him, honor and enjoy Him, our bond takes on the soft patina of a tried and enduring relationship.

Prayer

Lord, my intimate Friend, You have created human beings with the ability to communicate with each other. This happens through words, facial expressions, voice tones, and body posture, to name a handful. And the more intimately we know someone, the easier it is to "pick up on" these cues. Similarly, the more intimately we know You (through prayer, meditation, study of Scripture, etc.), the easier it is to recognize Your voice, Your prompting in our spirits. You go to great lengths to have a covenant relationship with each of Your children. Help us to have full appreciation for how transforming it is to be in personal connection with You. Guide us to be responsive to ways we can nurture that connection.

More scriptures to employ and enjoy

Psalm 17:8; 119:2

Jeremiah 24:7

Matthew 10:30

Isaiah 44:24; 49:16

James 4:8

Chapter 38

Who touched Me? Luke 8:45 (NLT)

A call to touch Jesus

Imagine a person has been in a locked room all his life –
no windows, no TV, phones or internet – zero link to the
outside world. One day some people try to describe to
this man what a tree looks like. They even draw a picture
and bring in a photograph. But it is impossible for the
man to fully appreciate a three-dimensional tree from
two-dimensional renditions. He may have an idea what
the tree looks like, but he can't know exactly, nor can he
experience its scents, texture, or sounds as the wind
swims among its leaves.

This is precisely why Jesus came – to destroy evil
(1 John 3:8), and to exhibit the power, love, and mercy of
God walking among us. Prior to the incarnation we had
prophets and visions and written words. But when the
Word was born into our world, when He took on a three-
dimensional flesh and blood body, He gave humankind
something upon which to cast its eyes, something to
hear, to touch.

When the sunshine streams through a window we don't actually see the light in and of itself but we do see all that it illuminates – a flower pot, chair, even dust particles hovering in midair. The light has a place to "land." That's Jesus – heaven's light beheld in an earthly body.

In the Bible scene containing this question, Jesus was barely able to move around as He was hemmed in by a large horde of people. Then, much to the amazement of His disciples, He asked, "Who touched Me?"

Peter answered, "Master, the people are crowding and pressing in on You!" – as if to imply, "there are **many** people touching You!" But, Jesus knew someone had touched Him with purpose and expectation for He said, "Someone deliberately touched Me, for I felt healing power go out from Me" (NLT).

When a woman came forth and confessed that she had been the one to touch Him, seeking a cure, Jesus replied, "Your faith has made you well" (verse 48).

Again, we are witness to the power of faith. Dozens, maybe hundreds, of others were pressing in around Him. **She** touched Him in faith. Can you and I have the kind of faith that draws the healing, restorative power from Jesus? Absolutely. Of course, right now we cannot reach out and touch Jesus with our physical hands but we can touch Him in a very real spiritual sense. Hebrews 4:16 tells us we have access to His throne. Our faith can go there – to the throne room of heaven – and actually touch Him.

Now, as the woman had to wind through a large, obstructive mass of people to get to our Savior, so we may have to do the same from a spiritual bearing. When we raise up our faith to Jesus in petition, we may need to push through our own "crowd" of distractions, unbelief, and other spiritual obstacles. But, we can remember the lesson of this woman not to give up. We are to keep pressing through in faith.

An interesting point about this episode is that it is really a story within a story. Jesus had been on His way to see the dying daughter of Jarius, a Jewish leader, when this woman dared to seek her healing. Notice Jesus didn't say, "I'm in a hurry. I must get to that little girl now!" No. Jesus took the time to find out who had touched Him and to give her words of encouragement: "Go in peace" (verse 48).

The Bible tells us that while He was still speaking to her, word came that the young girl had died. At this moment it looked as if the "diversion" of the Lord's attention was fatal to the child, but Jesus knew the girl would live and He instructed her father to trust Him.

I see this delay, though by appearances, deadly for the young girl, as a faith-booster for her father. He was able to witness the restoration of health and well-being to this woman, and right before he would get word of his child's death. So, when Jesus told him not to fear wouldn't we suppose those words now could be a sanctuary of hope for him?

The point I find so fascinating is this: Jesus, on a crucial life and death mission, was not too busy to speak with a woman about healing for another health issue, certainly not a grave matter for she'd been bothered by it for 12 years. This assures us God is never too busy to talk with us, never too preoccupied with larger and loftier matters. Our concerns, great and small, are important to Him.

Throughout His time on earth, Jesus used parables, real-life illustrations, to teach: the wind to explain the rebirth (John 3:8); the Good Samaritan (Luke 10:30-37) to demonstrate human compassion; and the farmer sowing seed (Luke 8:4-15), the ten virgins (Matthew 25:1-13), the silver pieces (Matthew 25:14-30), the wedding banquet (Matthew 22:2-14), the pearl (Matthew 13:44-46), and the mustard seed (Luke 13:18-19) to depict the reign of God.

Through His words, His body, His life, He has made the kingdom of God accessible, understandable, tangible, touchable.

"Who touched Me?" He asks.

Can we answer in faith, "Me, Lord"?

Prayer

Touchable Lord, You are always within our reach. May we behold, in the powerful words of the Gospels, how You welcomed those reaching out to You. And even though we can't see You today with our physical eyes or touch You with our earthly hands, how inexpressibly wonderful it is that we can approach the throne room of grace and, there, touch You with our faith, hope, and expectancy.

More scriptures to enjoy and employ

Romans 1:20

Colossians 2:9

1 John 5:14-15

Mark 10:13-16

John 3:19; 8:12

2 Corinthians 4:4

Ephesians 5:8

Chapter 39

Children, have you caught anything to eat?
John 21:5 (AMP)

A call to obedience

I remember one morning years ago when my husband and son were preparing for an out-of-town golf trip. I always pray for my family members when they go somewhere, but this day I sensed a strong prompting to pray against drunk driving. I did and enjoyed peace the rest of the day. That evening, when my husband and son arrived home they were visibly shaken and proceeded to tell this story: It seems an intoxicated man driving a pick-up truck flew recklessly out of the parking lot of a bar right into the middle of a busy intersection. He slammed into several cars, each time either spinning around or backing up and smashing into another. It was like a scene from a destruction derby. The sounds of screams, squealing tires, and metal grinding on metal filled the air. Then, all of a sudden, the reeling pick-up came to a stop facing our vehicle. It looked as if it would be the next target. With traffic all around, there was nowhere for them to go. The truck revved and lurched forward towards our car. Then, the hand of God moved. The pick-up's door latched onto the door of an adjacent car, which pulled it off course. As the crazed driver tried to gun forward, his truck veered to the side, encumbered and off-balance by the attached automobile.

No one will ever convince me that this deliverance was anything other than God's divine protection over my family. I am so thankful that He led me to pray and that I obeyed. His persuasions, in my experience, are persistent and very tender.

When Elijah took shelter in a cave in 1 Kings 19, he witnessed a crushing wind, an earthquake, and, finally, a fire. But the Lord was not present in any of these phenomena. Instead, He spoke to Elijah in a still, whispering voice – "a sound of gentle blowing" (verse 12).

At our church last weekend a visiting pastor from Kenya described his ride from the airport. With his thick accent he expressed amazement at the GPS on the dashboard of the car, directing the driver. With a sweet naivete he gushed, "The little box talked!" What stories this man will tell back home!

Indeed, those global positioning systems are good little guides to keep us on track – or to get us back on the right road should we take a wrong turn. The breath of the Holy Spirit is a GPS, as well (God's Positioning System).

Have you ever felt a prompting in your spirit – that gentle whispering sound? Maybe it was beckoning you to pray for someone, to do something, to say something, even to resist saying something. At times these might seem easily dismissible, but in our commitment to God and our acknowledgement of His superior wisdom, we obey, and later we may discover just how critical they really were. Further, the positive effects of many more of our acts of compliance may not be fully revealed to us this side of heaven.

The Bible is home to example after example of the need for obedience. We remember the story of Jonah. If this prophet had heeded God's first instructions to travel to Nineveh to preach against the wickedness there, he would not have found himself in a fish's belly for three days. Who can overlook the exploits of the Israelites who wandered 40 years in the desert because they refused to obey God's order to enter the Promised Land? And let us not neglect to mention the act of disobedience in the Garden of Eden that effectuated the fall of man.

The cost of disobedience can be high − so high, in fact, that it took a sweeping, gut-wrenching act of obedience from God's Son to pay that price.

Our opening question appears in a scene where experienced fishermen had been fishing all night long without success. Jesus appeared and asked them, "Children, have you caught anything to eat?" When they replied, "Not a thing," He directed them to cast their net off the starboard side. We read that they didn't even have to move the boat! Now, we must also consider that this incident took place subsequent to Jesus' resurrection and the disciples did not yet recognize Who He was. Perhaps they wondered, "Who is this guy telling professionals how to do our job?" As always, though, Jesus spoke with the authority and wisdom of God. The men were obedient and we know the rest of the story. What a catch came their way! Their nets were filled beyond what should have been the bursting point.

How often we "experienced," "worldly" people are certain that we know the correct way of doing things. We'll remember the telling passage in Haggai 1:5-7 discussed in chapter seven where the Lord addresses the governor of Judah and the high priest, urging them to consider their ways. For us today, in light of what has transpired in our lives − in a general or more specific sense − is God trying to get our attention and plead,

"Consider your ways"? I do not suggest that behaviors and choices are the provenance of all conditions and circumstances we meet, but if what we're doing isn't working, if our ways are not producing intended results, it may be time to prayerfully contemplate another approach, seek a new direction. And we need not be surprised if the Lord leads us to a course of action that just doesn't seem to accommodate any worldly logic at all. Proverbs 3:5-6 (NLT) assures us: "Trust in the Lord with all your heart; do not depend on your own understanding. Seek His will in all you do, and He will show you which path to take."

How many of us grew up hearing from our parents, "Because I said so"? Maybe we even find ourselves echoing that phrase back to our own children. Exasperating as it might be to a youngster with a bushelful of questions, it is a simple matter of a more experienced judgment being in control.

Obedience to God is propped by the twin pillars of humility and discipline. We are displaying humility when our heart-compass continually points to the polestar of God. Discipline entails following through on something just because it is right, regardless of feelings. When we are obedient to the Lord, despite what we feel we want or may think is best, we are setting ourselves up for favorable outcomes because we have the advantage of relying on wisdom infinitely superior to our own (see Isaiah 55:8-9).

A good parent demands obedience from a child. That child may throw fits and tantrums but a loving parent holds firm for the sake of the child's well-being and best interests.

We'll notice that following their act of obedience, not only were Jesus' disciples richly blessed, but also they came to recognize Him. Obedience brings about lucidity because we are led along the God-intended path.

This truth is heralded in John 14:21 (NLT): "Those who accept My commandments and obey them are the ones who love Me. And because they love Me, My Father will love them. And I will love them and reveal myself to each of them."

"Children, have you caught anything to eat?" Just beyond our topic question, within this same gospel story, our Lord issues three directives:

Cast your net (verse 6),

Bring Me the fish you caught (verse 10), and

Come and eat your meal (verse 12).

These sum up the obedience-blessing continuum. What is interesting is that even before the disciples brought Him their catch, Jesus already had fish cooking and bread at the ready. In a scene reminiscent of the Last Supper, He took the bread and fish and gave them to His disciples (verse 13). He did not need their catch but He did need their obedience, for they were about to pilot His ministry of salvation without the benefit of His physical presence. It would be imperative that they carry on that mission not according to human, worldly considerations, but in deference to the supernatural tenor of God's kingdom.

Ultimately, obedience means we love God and trust Him beyond our own wisdom and point of view. It means we are secure enough in faith and humble enough in attitude that we will do what He tells us whether or not it seems rational to our natural minds.

I conclude this chapter by sharing a fitting story I heard years ago. It seems a ferocious storm struck a small farming town. When a local farmer ventured outside to secure his animals in the barn he noticed some beautiful birds struggling in the strong winds and hail. He tried to wave them into the safety of the barn but his wild gestures and hollering only added to their panic and confusion.

"Oh," the farmer lamented, "if only I could become one of them for just a short time."

Finally, after repeated attempts to help the birds failed, he had to close the barn door for the sake of his own animals. Head down, he fought his way through the torrent back to his house.

The next day dawned calmer. As the farmer walked towards the barn a dreadful sight met his eyes. The gorgeous birds lay lifeless on the ground – so close to what could have been their refuge. The farmer knew that if he could have put his wisdom into "bird form" the others would have followed him inside the barn to safety.

Our Father has done that for us in Christ. His peerless, preeminent wisdom embodied in our Savior beckons us to follow and obey. And, as we've seen, this obedience brings protection, revelation, blessings, and the grand opportunity to be used by God in the advancement of His plans.

Prayer

All-knowing, All-seeing, All-powerful One, being led by anything or anyone other than You is folly and foolishness. I am Your servant and I want You to know You can count on me. Guide me to obedience that is pleasing to You in the little things and the big.

More scriptures to enjoy and employ

1 John 3:22

Psalm 103:18; 112:1; 119:145-146

Joshua 24:24

Romans 1:5; 6:17; 16:26

1 Peter 1:2,14

Isaiah 1:19; 50:10

1 Samuel 15:22

Proverbs 25:12

Acts 5:29

Hebrews 5:9

Jeremiah 7:22-23; 11:7

John 15:14

Deuteronomy 5:29; 8:1

Luke 5:4-6; 6:46

Chapter 40

Do you love Me?   John 21:15-17

*A call to love God and show
it by serving others*

There are people who travel from city to city, football game to football game, to raise placards from the crowd which simply read: "John 3:16." This verse contains the core message of our faith – Christianity in a nutshell, so to speak. God so loved that He gave His Son (that's His part), so that whoever believes (our part) has eternal life (the reward).

Love is a word with many layers of meaning. We can love a lasagna dinner, a favorite song, or a relaxing back massage. People may fall in or out of love multiple times. But, how does the Bible define love? 1 Corinthians 13:13 (AMP) phrases it this way: "true affection for God and man, growing out of God's love for us and in us." (More on this momentarily.)

Jesus asked Peter the question, "Do you love Me?" three distinct times, perhaps to allow him to spiritually bury his three-part denial. And after each affirmative response by Peter, the Lord gave a command:

"Tend My lambs,"

"Shepherd My sheep," and finally,

"Tend My sheep."

It was by Peter's profession of love that Jesus knew he would act, he would give, he would take on the role of shepherd. For genuine love simply MUST give. We can give without loving, but it is not possible to love without giving.

We discussed faith in chapters three, eight, and nine, and hope in chapter 32. Love completes the heavenly "tripod" we read about in 1 Corinthians 13:13: "But now faith, hope, love, abide these three. And the greatest of these is love." It is the greatest because God is love. It is His very nature. It is Who He is. It is what He does. It is why we're here.

Love acts. God *loves* so He *gave*.

Endorheic bodies of water have tributaries but no drains (other than evaporation and seepage). The Dead Sea is one such entity. It receives but it does not give. As a result, minerals and pollutants collect in high concentrations, rendering its waters virtually uninhabitable. We receive God's love and when we, in turn, allow that love to circulate through us and into the worlds of others, the waters of our spirits will teem with life.

This returns us to our biblical definition of love – that it begins with God's love for us. We might consider this the very first rung on a ladder of spiritual progression:

He first loved us (1 John 3:1).

Because He first loved us we love Him and have the same love for one another (1 John 4:11,19).

When we love one another God dwells in us (1 John 4:12).

With love (God) in us there is no room for fear (1 John 4:18; 2 Timothy 1:7; Psalm 118:6).

When fear is gone, faith has room to grow (Mark 4:40; 5:36; Hebrews 13:5-6).

When faith takes over, it is pleasing to God (Hebrews 11:6).

When we please God, our prayers are answered! (1 John 3:22).

Along our climb up this "love ladder," not only are our neighbors loved and served, but God is honored and pleased and, as a happy by-product, our own faith and prayers become more effective. We have favor.

Consider this: I love my children so much that even when I see someone who looks like or reminds me of them in some way, I feel a special "tug." Without knowing anything else about them, I might act more favorably towards these individuals simply because they resemble my kids.

Now, there is no partiality with God (Ephesians 6:9), and no doubt He considers all of us His sons and daughters. Further, I'm quite certain physical appearances are not a priority with Him. However, when we look like His Son, Jesus (and since God has His eye upon the heart, we never look more like Jesus than when we are loving others), I believe we enjoy a particular privilege of our Father's affection.

When meeting a newborn, delighted friends and relatives often gush forth comments such as, "Oh, she looks just like her dad!" "He has his father's nose and his mother's smile." "She wrinkles her nose just like Grandpa!" It can be fun to see certain familial resemblances, traits, and strengths wend their way through the generations. When we are "born" into God's family, our resemblance to Him is apparent as we display the fruits of the Spirit, most notably love.

There is tremendous significance in Jesus' asking this question just prior to departing earth for heaven. As His *literal* body was about to ascend, He knew the torch of God's message must continue to burn in Peter and the church, and in His followers, present and future – in other words, His *figurative* body.

In some masterfully designed way, this question, "Do you love Me?" is all-inclusive, dovetailing every last one of the 39 others in a compact package of four small words. For, one who loves will, synchronously, be about His Father's business, show mercy, compassion, kindness, trust, integrity, and gratitude. He will live a fruitful and focused life, be quick to repent, non-judgmental, hopeful, obedient, and steadfast (and on and on).

Jesus did not say His disciples would be known by their fancy church buildings, religious jewelry, or how many passages they highlight in their Bibles. He said they would be known by their love. When all is said and done, the one who meets the criteria to be called a true ambassador for Jesus Christ is, very simply, one who loves.

<u>Prayer</u>

God, Lover of my soul, the purest, cleanest water is that which continuously runs a course. Help me remember always that I am not just a receptacle of Your love, but a channel. Your church was founded on love. I desire to continue this mission by serving others. Guide me to see the needs of those around me and creative ways to help and encourage – not for earthly kudos and reward, but to gladden You, to be more like Your Son, and to care for those for whom Your Son died. Let me not be satisfied with just "talking the talk." May I "walk the walk."

<u>More scriptures to enjoy and employ</u>

James 2:15-17

1 Peter 4:8

1 Timothy 1:5

1 Thessalonians 3:12

Luke 6:27

1 John 4:9

Matthew 25:31-40

Colossians 3:14

John 13:35; 15:13

1 Corinthians 4:19-20

Ephesians 3:17

About the Author

Lori and her husband live among the grapevines of Napa Valley and have two grown children and four grandchildren. She tutors middle school and high school math and considers herself a life-long student of Scripture. In addition to Liguori Publications, her work has appeared in numerous publications including *The Family*, *Kid Konnection, Pennywhistle Press, Sunday Digest, Highlights for Children, Jack and Jill, and Evangel.* In a project that combined her love for teaching and her heart for Scripture, she helped create Bible-based lesson plans for children's Sunday school classes for Treasure Publishing.

Printed in Dunstable, United Kingdom

77196486R10127